THE PHANTOM CONFLICT

Produced by Raymond Creed,
Director of *'Rebuild Christianity Publications'* and the *'Rebuild Christianity'* web site at www.rebuildchristianity.com

Author of: -

'Facing the Unthinkable'

'The Fifty-Two Attributes of God'

'The Leeds Liturgy'

Storefront
http://stores.lulu.com/rebuildchristianity or
http://stores.lulu.com/store.php?fAcctID=976144

Copies of soft cover editions may also be available through Amazon and other International Distributors

THE PHANTOM CONFLICT

(Bible teaching on the relationship between divine holiness and divine love in connection with Christian idolatry and the need for a balanced Christian life)

Revelation 4:8
"And the four [angelic] *beasts had each of them six wings about him and they were full of eyes within and they rest not day and night, saying, 'Holy, Holy, Holy, Lord God Almighty, who was and is and is to come.'"*

Thought Starter
"Neglect God's holiness and the result is laxity, Neglect God's love and the result is legalism."[1]

Raymond Creed

Rebuild Christianity Publications
www.rebuildchristianity.com

---

[1] The author, Thursday 11th November 1999

Produced by Raymond Creed,
Director of *'Rebuild Christianity Publications'* and the *'Rebuild Christianity'* web site at www.rebuildchristianity.com

Published by Rebuild Christianity Publications

Copyright © the Author 2010
(Backdated to cover all material produced by the author before 2010)

All Rights Reserved,
The Moral Right of the author has been asserted.

First (Pilot) Edition 2009, limited distribution only is now out of print

Second (International) Edition 2010, should be available through international distributors like Amazon

ISBN: 978-1-907910-02-9

Contents

Introduction VII

Preface: Dismal Swamps VIII

Explanation of Terminology X

Prologue: Are You Willing? XV

C1: Thematic Bible Expositions **1**

S1: God's Holiness and Divine Inapproachability in the Old Testament 3

S2: God's Holiness and Divine Inapproachability in the New Testament 6

S3: God's Love and Divine Approachability in the Old Testament 10

S4: God's Love and Divine Approachability in the New Testament 13

S5: Deviant Forms of Christianity 17

C2: Midrash Bible Expositions **27**

S1: Homiletic Midrash 29

S2: Parashiyot Midrash 31

S3: Peshar Midrash 34

C3: Analysis and Application **41**

S1: A Dynamic Relationship 43

S2: The Blessing of Balance 46

S3: Idols in the Heart 49

Conclusion **57**

Appendices: Confessional and Other Summaries **65**

A1: Biblical Teaching on Divine Holiness and Divine Love 67

A2: Question and Answer Summary 70

A3: Confessional Summary 76

A4: Mathematical Summary 80

A5: Test Summary 82

Selective Bibliography **85**

S1: Book List 87

S2: Reference Works 89

S3: Other Information Sources 90

Titles by the Same Author **91**

Facing the Unthinkable 93

The 52 Attributes of God 94

The Leeds Liturgy 95

Key

A: Appendix

C: Chapter

S: Section

Introduction

'The Phantom Conflict' endeavours to rebuild Christianity by showing how a balanced emphasis between divine holiness and divine love is a necessary prerequisite for healthy Christian living. The problem of Christian idolatry is also tackled.

'The Phantom Conflict' addresses the following questions: -
1) How does divine holiness relate to divine love?
2) How is it possible to avoid incorrect views of God?
3) How is it possible to avoid idolatry?

'The Phantom Conflict,' assumes that correct ideas of God are a vital precondition to spiritual fruitfulness. It argues that to exaggerate divine holiness at the expense of divine love (or vice-versa) produces a warped and ineffective version of Christianity. At one extreme it becomes a religion of fear and at the other a religion of flippancy. Both deviations harm their adherents and discredit the gospel.

This book should prove particularly useful to religious ministers (of all denominational backgrounds), local church elders, Christian teachers, evangelists and theological students. The Messianic Jewish community and those wishing to delve deeper into theology would also benefit.

'The Phantom Conflict' serves as a practical and interactive teaching tool, being divided into easily accessible sections, all undergirded by ancient Jewish methods of bible interpretation (*'Midrash'*). It may be regarded as an independent work or as a successor volume to *'The 52 Attributes of God.'*

Readers who do not wish to know how this book came to be written should skip the preface.

To purchase a download, hard or soft cover edition please visit: -

http://stores.lulu.com/rebuildchristianity or

http://stores.lulu.com/store.php?fAcctID=976144

Soft cover editions may also be available through Amazon and other International Distributors.

Preface: Dismal Swamps

Tozer (1976)[2] once made the accurate observation that, *"it might be demonstrated that almost every heresy that has afflicted the Church through the years has arisen from believing about God things that are not true, or from over-emphasizing certain true things so as to obscure other things equally true. To magnify any attribute to the exclusion of another is to head straight for one of the dismal swamps of theology; and yet we are all constantly tempted to do just that."*

This is precisely what has happened in recent decades in many Western Churches, where an over emphasis upon divine love has led to a denial of divine holiness. One result has been a widespread crisis of powerlessness and Christian ineffectiveness – with the Church losing the capacity to resist even overt and obvious deceptions.[3] *'The Phantom Conflict'* employs scripture to interpret divine holiness and divine love so that both are equally and boldly affirmed; only a *'phantom conflict'* exists between them. In correcting this common misapprehension about God, Christians should become liberated to lead lives truly honouring to Him.

Hopefully, the reader will come to appreciate: -
1) How important it is to have a clear idea of who God is
2) The strong relationship existing between divine holiness and divine love
3) How confusion concerning God's attributes leads to an ineffective Christian life
4) How God's power unites divine holiness and divine love
5) How ancient Jewish methods of bible interpretation resolve apparently contradictory bible passages
6) How divine perfection rules out conflict within God Himself
7) How divine power enhances rather than diminishes human characteristics *i.e.* the ability to think, feel, socialise and make decisions
8) The challenge of loving God before anything else

---

[2] Gems of Tozer, p.13
[3] One of these being the Prosperity Gospel which teaches that all Christians have an automatic right to *'health and wealth;'* gained through various *'Positive Thinking'* techniques.

One assumption under-girding this study is the belief that correct ideas about the Deity act as a *'necessary,'* although not a *'sufficient'* cause of spiritual fruitfulness at both the individual and corporate level. We can only bear the *'right fruit'* in the service of Christ if we possess a reasonably clear idea of <u>who God is.</u> Any confusion about His attributes tends only to end in a frustrating ineffectiveness. Being stuck in *'the dismal swamps of theology'* is an unpleasant experience; we either sink or come out smelling!

Some of the material for this work was originally presented in the form of an essay for a certain Bible College during the final quarter of 1992 whilst the writer was studying for a Diploma in Theology as an external student. The need to rewrite, restructure and amend key points led to it being substantially reworked during the period of late 1998 until early 1999. It was around that time the following meditation spoke to me: -

The Lord is holy
The Lord is pure
The Lord is inapproachable
He is infinitely separate from anything profane

Only a fool will try to approach the Lord
Trusting in their paltry strength or supposed righteousness!

Yet, in His love, God sent His Only Son Jesus,
Who 'came in the flesh' to save us from our sin
Only through His blood sacrifice may we approach the Lord
And avoid the wrath that is our due[4]

Until October 2009, *'The Phantom Conflict'* formed *'Part B'* of *'The Fifty-two Attributes of God'* which was then entitled *'About God.'* Further corrections were made in December 2009, February 2010 and October-November 2010. By this stage, this work had gone well beyond its original essay form and was ready for international distribution on book form.

Summary tables listing the bible passages referring to both divine holiness and to divine love will be found in **Appendix 1.**

The Author: Thursday, 9th December 2010

---

[4] Entitled *'No One'* it was first written on Monday, 8th February 1999. It expresses the need to appreciate both divine holiness and divine love.

Explanation of Terminology

A: Terms Concerning God and His Attributes

1) Almighty
God's total power: His unlimited strength and boundless capacity to govern everything He has made. None of His plans fail. It is expressed in His powerful ability to hold together such apparently diverse characteristics as holiness and love. In scripture, God is frequently referred to as the *'Almighty,'* which means *'all powerful One.'* The effect of God's almighty power enhances such human attributes as will, reason, emotion and the ability to relate to others. In other words, the operation of divine power makes people more human and enhances their individuality.[5]

2) Attribute Linkage
The bonds which unite one attribute to another. The presence of such links allows for a positive relationship to exist between divine holiness and divine love.[6]

3) Attribute Misfocus
A condition which occurs where divine one attribute is emphasised at the expense of another; for example, a person or group may focus upon God's holiness and not upon His love or vice-versa. When this happens a negative relationship is assumed to exist between these two attributes.

4) Divine Holiness
God's total purity: His morally upright freedom and separation from any trace of corruption and His hostile repugnance to every form of evil. This total purity renders Him unapproachable to mortal human beings and is expressed in His wrathful punishment of sinners. There is no positive relationship at all between God and sinful humanity, even though the latter may try hard to earn that relationship with Him through moralistic self-effort or religious practice. Such efforts would never be *'good enough'* to bridge the gap between God and humanity nor to placate God's wrath against sin.

---

[5] This is in direct contrast to *'Satanic'* power which tends to dehumanise people by robbing them of their individual personality. The writer noticed this effect when observing manifestations of the Toronto Deception during the mid-1990s.

[6] One example of an attribute linkage is the way divine power gives God the unlimited capacity needed to unite divine holiness and love. Another is divine peace which allows for such a unity without any conflict or internal disorder.

5) Divine Love

God's total compassion: His rational, selfless, tender and unlimited kindness, directed to all of His Creation. It engenders a gracious pity toward those who do not know Him and motivates Him to approach and reveal Himself to mortal human beings. Divine love is expressed in God's merciful forgiveness of sinners. The term *'holy-love'* emphasises the purity and moral uprightness found within divine love. Because of God's utter holiness people are debarred from reaching Him. However, the Almighty is not debarred from reaching people – once the offering of an unblemished sacrifice has totally satisfied the requirements of divine holiness. Such a sacrifice makes God approachable to those who would put their trust in Him.

6) God

The completely perfect, personal, supreme spiritual Being who possesses an unlimited number of interrelated, non-conflicting attributes; He can think, feel, decide and relate to others in a highly sociable way. In this latter context, it's worth noting God's: -

6.1 Approachability, His total accessibility to those members of the human race whose sins have been atoned for (covered over) by an unblemished sacrifice.[7]

6.2 Inpproachability, His total inaccessibility to those members of the human race whose sins have not been atoned for (covered over) by an unblemished sacrifice.

7) One

A complex, compound or pluralistic unity rather than a simple, elemental or indivisible unity; it corresponds to the Hebrew word *'Echad'* (meaning pluralistic oneness) rather than *'Yachid'* (meaning simple oneness). This *'pluralistic oneness'* consists of: -

7:1 An Essential Unity (Oneness): a unity acting as a link between all of God's attributes (perfect characteristics) – including holiness and love.

7:2 A Personal Unity (Oneness): a unity existing between the divine Three Persons constituting God Himself – the Father, Son and Holy Spirit. This unity is often referred to as the *'Trinity'* (tri-unity).[8]

---

[7] A sacrifice that will have appeased divine wrath and fully constituted the requirements of divine holiness; Christ's death upon the cross constituted just such a sacrifice. However, any benefits from this sacrifice become operational only where a real and continuing faith in Christ exists.

[8] For reasons of space the focus will be upon the *'essential'* rather than the *'personal'* oneness of God.

XII

8) Lord
Revered, Sovereign Master; having connotations with *'ownership,'* it emphasises the fact that God owns and is sovereign Master over everything He has made. Akin to scripture, this study uses the term *'God'* interchangeably with *'Lord.'*

9) The Essentialist Model
A model of God presupposing divine attributes like holiness and love are essential to one-another; a harmonious and positive relationship is seen to exist between them; this means that it is legitimate to speak of God's *'holy-love'* without contradicting scripture[9].

10) The Oppositionist Model
A model of God presupposing divine attributes like holiness and love are opposed to one-another; a conflict or negative relationship is seen to exist between them. Often tacitly accepted rather than militantly proclaimed, this model leads quite naturally to the problem of attribute misfocus.

B: Terms Concerning Methodology

1) The Affirmative Method
A method which scrutinises a particular viewpoint by asking, *"What are the likely logical and practical consequences of affirming this particular teaching?"*

2) The Bradford Method
A method in algebraic form which expresses the relationship between various Biblical teachings; it puts forward a balanced view of biblical truth, so reducing the risk of over emphasising some doctrines at the expense of others.

3) The Denial Method:
A method which scrutinises a particular viewpoint by asking, *"What are the likely logical and practical consequences of denying this particular teaching?"*

4) The Interactive Method
A method which discovers the inter-relationship between particular Biblical teachings, showing how they support and confirm one another; it asks, *"How do the attributes of divine holiness and divine*

---

[9] This model is often quietly ignored rather than militantly rejected in the Church.

love interact with one other?" It can also be used in conjunction with either *'The Affirmative'* or *'The Denial Method.'*

C: Terms Concerning Midrash

1) Midrash
The Jewish method of interpreting scripture as used by Jesus and the Apostles; the word *'Midrash'* derives from the Hebrew word *'Daresh'* meaning *'to make a rigorous investigation of.'*

2) Homiletic Midrash:
A form of Midrash offering simple doctrinal instruction; it consists of four-parts: -
2.1 An introductory formula *e.g. 'As it is written'*
2.2 A collection of diverse Bible passages, used to illustrate a key theme
2.3 A commentary showing how these passages explain and clarify the major theme under scrutiny
2.4 A final conclusion, summing up the key points and encouraging practical application
An example of a Homiletic Midrash can be found in Romans 3:9-20.

3) Parashiyot Midrash
A complex form of Midrash, used to resolve apparent contradictions in scripture. It consists of: -
3.1 An introduction to the main theme
3.2 A standard <u>introductory</u> phrase at key points *e.g. 'It is contained in the scripture'*
3.3 The Petkah (or <u>base</u> passage) followed by a running commentary
3.4 An opposing, <u>intersecting</u> (apparently contradictory) Bible passage, again with a running commentary
3.5 A final <u>concluding</u> (or reconciling) passage, followed by a brief commentary and resolving the apparent contradiction
3.6 Practical instruction (which may also include re-quotations and other Biblical material)
An example of a Parashiyot Midrash can be found in 1 Peter 2:4f.

4) Peshar Midrash
A still more complex form of Midrash, comprising of: -
4.1 A main (sometimes long or paraphrased) Bible quotation.
4.2 An exegesis (simple exposition) which usually includes: -
4.2.1 Smaller re-quotes from the main passage

4.2.2 Quotations from other scriptures[10]
4.2.3 A practical application (which may also include re-quotations and other Biblical material)
An example of a Peshar Midrash can be found in Hebrews 3:1-4:11 (and also in 7:1-8:5).

5) Running Commentary
A brief commentary highlighting the main points made by a particular (often very small) passage of scripture; little (if any) context is given.

6) Thematic Bible Study
A form of study wherein a large number of scripture references are gathered together to provide in-depth coverage of one particular theme (or teaching) found present throughout the Bible. Such references may be quoted, cited or only generally alluded to. They may also be accompanied by running commentaries.

Comments

Faith in God may be expressed in a whole variety of ways, including through *'creeds,' 'confessions* and *'catechisms.'* Here: -
- A *'creed'* is a concisely expressed *'statement of belief'* arranged in logical order.
- A *'confession of faith'* has the same function as a *'creed'* but is expressed itself in a longer prose form and is often accompanied by detailed explanations of why a given *'belief'* is true.
- A *'catechism'* uses an interactive *'question and answer'* format and can be geared to different levels of understanding.

All three are valuable teaching tools and for this reason, **Appendices 2** and **3** consist of a *'catechism'* and a *'confession.'*[11]

---

[10] These other scriptural quotations are cited in order to apply Deuteronomy 19:15 and to reinforce the main line of argument.
[11] Examples of Creeds can be found in the writer's devotional work *"The Leeds Liturgy'* (2010).

Prologue: Are You Willing?

*Are you willing to love God
With that rational, self-giving 'agape' love
Which reaches out to Him?*

*Are you willing to love God
In a self-sacrificial way,
Placing obedience to His will above every other consideration?*

*Are you willing to love God
With that love which cries, 'Abba, Father?'*

*Are you willing to love God
With that love which declares, 'Jesus Christ is Lord,
He 'came in the flesh' to die for my sin?'*[12]

*Are you willing to love God
With that love outpoured by the Holy Spirit?*

*Are you willing to love God
In the face of difficulty, rejection and persecution -
Even from those who call themselves Christians?*

*Are you willing to love God
At the very moment of death?*

*Are you willing to love God
By worshipping Him forever
With all of your heart, mind and soul?*

*If you are, then receive that strength
To love the God of holy-love,
Have fellowship with Him
And <u>enjoy</u> His invigorating presence*[13]

---

[12] See John 1:14 & 1 John 4:1-3

[13] This devotional came to mind on Wednesday, 8th December 1998 whilst walking to a particular city centre through a thick grey mist. It was drafted that very same day. It expresses the need to accept the challenge to love the God of holy-love. Should anyone wish to respond to this then all they need say is, *"Yes Lord, I am willing to love you with that kind of love, Amen."*

Questions

1) Why does God seem to have certain times when He challenges His people to love Him? How can people respond to that challenge and practice that love in everyday life?

2) To what extent do you agree (or disagree) with the view which states, *'One of the hardest things in the Christian life is to go on loving God in the face of great suffering and personal failure.'*

3) Does the meditation *'Are you willing?'* proffer a false *'salvation by works,'* where God draws close only to those who would follow Him wholeheartedly?

C1:

THEMATIC BIBLE EXPOSITIONS

2

S1: God's Holiness and Divine Inapproachability in the Old Testament

The strong relationship existing between God's holiness and divine inapproachability is revealed throughout the Old Testament in a variety of ways: -

1) God's own character
Leviticus 20:3, 22:32; 1 Chronicles 16:35; Psalms 103:1, 111:9; Isaiah 52:10; Hosea 11:9 & Amos 4:2

2) Explicit divine titles; one of these being *'the Holy One of Israel'*
2 Kings 19:22; Psalms 71:22, 78:41, 89:18; Isaiah 1:4, 5:19 & 24, 10:20, 37:23, 43:3 & 14 & 16 & 20, 45:11; Jeremiah 50:29, 51:5 & Ezekiel 39:7

3) Other divine attributes, including: -
- Goodness – Isaiah 57:13; Ezekiel 20:9 & Hosea 11:9
- Majesty – Exodus 15:11; 1 Samuel 2:2, 6:20; Isaiah 6:3 & 10:7
- Wrath – Exodus 22:24, 32:10; 2 Chronicles 28:11; Ezra 10:14; Psalm 78:31; John 3:36; Romans 1:18; Ephesians 5:6; Colossians 3:6; Revelation 14:10 & 19, 15:1, 7, 16:1 & 19:15

4) Explicit divine commands
Leviticus 11:45

5) Specific divine works, including: -
- Answering prayer – Psalms 3:4, 20:6 & 28:2
- Deliverance – Psalms 22:2-4, 89:18, 103:1, 105:3, 142:21; Isaiah 6:3, 10:20, 29:23-24, 49:7, 52:10; Jeremiah 5:5; Ezekiel 36:23 & 39:7
- Purifying people – Exodus 31:13; Leviticus 16:32, 20:8, 21:8 & 15 & :22-23

6) True, God-given religious experiences
Exodus 19:1f; Isaiah 6:1-5 & Ezekiel 1:1f

Exodus 19:21f will be looked at in more depth. A simple commentary will accompany each relevant citation.[14]

---
[14] The following pattern constitutes a very basic Midrash with quotations from scripture and a brief commentary.

The setting is Mount Sinai where the Lord has appeared before all of the Israelite tribes. In obedience to the Lord's command, Moses has gone up to the mountain to receive further instruction.

21. *"And the Lord said to Moses, 'Go down and warn the people, lest they break through to the Lord in order to gaze and many of them perish."*

This verse establishes the principle that <u>no sinful person can look upon the Lord and live.</u> Unless one's own moral pollution has been dealt with in some way, any meeting with God will have fatal consequences. Divine holiness produces a physical as well as a moral separation between God and humanity. <u>The One who is totally perfect in His holiness cannot abide, for one instant, the least trace of sin in any of His creatures.</u> Such imperfection always engenders an outbreak divine wrath, (which is the active expression of outraged holiness.)

22. *"And let the priests also, which come near to the Lord, sanctify* [dedicate and purify] *themselves, lest the Lord break forth upon them* [in His wrath].*"*

Even the high priests themselves, (who were supposed to be close to God) had to take care not to offend the Lord's holiness. It was made clear to them that <u>God, who is totally perfect, will never compromise His perfection, either by reducing His lofty moral standards or by allowing anything tainted by sin to enter His presence.</u> Indeed, if God allowed such things He would be sacrificing His own perfection – thereby immediately ceasing to be divine. It is essential to remember that, by definition, God is perfect. This means that He is complete in Himself and free from any fault or trace of sin in everything He thinks, says and does.

23. *"And Moses said unto the Lord, 'the people cannot come up to Mount Sinai because you have warned us, saying 'set boundaries around the Mount and sanctify it.'"*

Divine holiness firmly places a definite barrier between people and God. Furthermore, <u>it is a barrier that can never be breached from the human side.</u> Thus, any attempt to ascend to the Almighty through meditation, good works and other religious practices is a tragic waste of time. <u>No person on earth has the capacity to ascend to God.</u> Divine holiness provokes God to remain distant, hidden and inapproachable. Unless the Lord Himself intervenes, there remains not the slightest chance of any constructive relationship between Himself as Creator and His created works, including humanity itself.

24. *"And the Lord said to him* [Moses], *'Away, get down, and you shall come up, you and Aaron with you. However, do not let the priests and people break through to come up to the Lord, lest He breaks forth* [in holy wrath] *upon them."*

Divine holiness places a definite barrier between all types of people and God. Akin to their fellow Israelites, the priests also had to keep their distance. This was the case even where the priesthood concerned was not steeped in the idolatrous practices of the surrounding nations. Represented here is God's resounding *'no'* to all man-made ways of approaching Him. This *'no'* principle applies even when the way concerned justifies itself through the use of bible-passages (which are often taken out of context). Any man-made attempt to approach God provokes God's anger because it is rooted in human pride. It represents humanity's (often works-based) attempt to *'break through and come up to the Lord.'* Implicit is a warning against any proud desire to *'ascend'* to the Lord through spiritual techniques and practices like meditation. All these things can ever do is to provoke divine wrath.[15]

25. *"So Moses went down to the people and spoke to them."*

Only God can *'break through'* the barrier between His holiness and human corruption. God's way of breaking through this barrier (between Himself and the Israelites) was to send down a mediator who would speak to them. This mediator was, of course, Moses, who even at his best, was only a dim foreshadow of that far greater Mediator who would descend from Heaven (rather than from a mountain). This greater mediator would bring mercy rather than Law; he would speak to all nations rather than to the tribes of Israel alone and He, unlike Moses, would never sin.

Overall, **Exodus 19:21f** demonstrates that the main effect of divine holiness is to create a terrible separation (or gulf) between God and sinful humanity. Unless the Lord personally cleanses us by His Holy

---

[15] One manifestation of this wrath is the way those who would commit this folly are often given over to the influence of evil spirits. The writer saw this happen with those caught up in Prosperity Teaching.

Spirit, <u>no person on earth could approach Him and live.</u> He remains a condemning judge, ready to destroy us because of our iniquities. Our whole relationship with Him is completely disordered. For their own sakes, many Christians need to recapture a sense of divine holiness otherwise they will become traumatised when they see God's holiness beginning to express itself in a series of terrible judgements, inflicted on both a rebellious world and an apostate Church. It is high time for many believers in Christ to awaken and face up to such realities. In the Western World especially, there's been far too much of an *'All you need is love'* religiosity. Such a pseudo-faith owes more to human wishful thinking than to Biblical revelation.

Questions

1) Why does God not *'soften'* His commandments to make it easier for people to approach Him?

2) What implications does divine holiness have for every world religion?

3) Briefly describe God's way of *'breaching (breaking through) the barrier'* between Himself and humanity.

4) Give reasons suggesting why it is necessary to recapture a sense of divine holiness

S2: God's Holiness and Divine Inapproachability in the New Testament

The strong relationship existing between God's holiness and divine inapproachability is revealed throughout the New Testament in a variety of ways: -

1) God's own character
Luke 1:49; 1 Peter 1:15-16; Revelation 4:8 & 6:10

2) God the Father
John 17:11 & 1 John 2:20

3) Jesus
John 8:46

4) The Holy Spirit
Matthew 3:11, 12:31-32; Mark 1:8, 12:36, 13:12; Luke 1:15, 35, 41, 67, 2:25, 4:1, 11:13, 12:10-12; John 1:33, 3:34, 7:39, 14:26, 15:26, 16:8, 14, 20:22; Acts 1:2, 5, 8, 2:4, 33, 38, 4:8, 31, 5:3, 32, 6:3, 5, 13, 7:51, 55, 8:15-19, 9:17, 31, 10:38, 44-48, 11:15-16, 24, 52, 13:2-4, 15:8, 28, 16:6, 19:2, 6, 20:23, 28:25; Romans 5:1-5, 8:9, 9:1, 10:14, 14:17, 15:13-16; 1 Corinthians 2:10-14, 3:16, 6:10, 19, & 12:3-11; 2 Corinthians 1:22, 3:18 5:5, 6:6 13:1-14; Ephesians 1:13, 23, 4:30; 1 Thessalonians 1:5-6, 4:8; 2 Thessalonians 3:13-15; 2 Timothy 1:14; Titus 3:5; Hebrews 3:7-9, 9:8, 14, & 10:15-17 & 29; 1 Peter 1:12; 2 Peter 2:7; 1 John 5:7 & Jude :20

4) Messianic titles, *e.g. 'the Holy One of God'*
Mark 1:24; Luke 4:34; Acts 3:14 & 4:27

Hebrews 7:22-26 will be looked at in more depth. As in the previous two sections a simple commentary will accompany each citation.

Immediately prior to this passage the unknown author has been comparing the inadequacies of the old Levitical Priesthood with the perfect Priesthood of Christ. The whole Book of Hebrews is more akin to a formal treatise rather than an informal letter. It was addressed to a demoralised Messianic Jewish congregation who was seriously considering a return to Judaism, which at least had the advantage of being a recognised religion within the Roman Empire. They urgently needed to regain a clear picture of the person and work of Jesus Christ, because their own faith had become stale.

22. *"By so much was Jesus made a surety* [guarantee] *of a better Testament* [a solemn and binding agreement made by God to Man]*."*

The previous study of **Exodus 19:21f** demonstrated that the Sinai revelation did nothing to allow people to approach God directly. Moreover, whilst the exposition of **Psalm 103:8-13** will confirm that God could assume the role of a compassionate Father, it did not explain <u>how He could assume that role without compromising His perfect holiness.</u> This present passage begins to remedy this through the provision *"of a better Testament"* in Jesus Christ. God can now interact with humanity and avoid any diminution of His own absolute holiness. Only through Jesus can sinful people approach a Holy God. Also, a Holy God can now approach sinful people but again, <u>only</u> through Jesus, His much beloved Son.

23. *"And they truly were many priests, because they were not allowed to continue by reason of death."*

Already in **Exodus 19:24**, the Lord had pointed out the inadequacy of the Levitical Priesthood in gaining access to God. Like all religious systems, the Priesthood was also subject to *'the law of sin and death.'* The sacrifices were finite, transitory and needed to be repeated because they were of limited benefit. Perhaps the purest form of religious expression will take place in Christ's millennial reign where He will personally instruct the world in true doctrine. Sadly, Revelation 20:7-9 shows that even this glorious era in human history will end in a final revolt where Satan will *"deceive the nations"* and besiege *"the camp of the Saints."* The millennial Kingdom, borne out of crisis will end in crisis. This shows that even perfect social conditions will not cure human antagonism against God.

24. *"But this Man, because He continues forever, has an unchangeable priesthood."*

In the role of priest, Jesus acts as a mediator between God and Humanity. In this eternal (never ending) office He represents imperfect people before God and a perfect God before people. This means that God can relate as *'father'* to people because He sees them through the perfection of Jesus. Their sins have been dealt with and *'filtered out,'* no longer bringing pollution to the divine presence. However, such a filtration takes place only when people have believed in Jesus as Lord and Saviour. <u>Should this trust in Christ be absent, sin remains.</u> As John 3:36 warns, *"The wrath of God remains"* [on them]. Hence, it is by faith in Jesus that God can be known as *'gracious father'* rather than *'condemning judge.'*

25. *"Wherefore He is able also to save them to the uttermost that come to God by Him seeing that He forever lives to make intercessions for them."*

The author has a high regard for the priestly office of Christ. It is an office characterised by prayer and the ability to save believers who are in desperate straits. No human being can, by self-effort, ascend to God. Any attempt to do so is the equivalent of trying to walk backwards across the universe. We cannot ascend to God because He is infinite and we are limited; also He is holy and we are sinful. However, Christ has descended from Heaven in order to make possible that which hitherto had been impossible. People can now *"come to God"* without any risk to their lives. No one need remain quaking at the foot of Mount Sinai – access to the Almighty is now thankfully and free. Sin no longer bars the way.

26. *"For such a High Priest became able to meet our need, one who is holy, harmless, undefiled, separate from sinners, and made higher than the Heavens."*

The greatest need people have is to enter into a relationship with God. However, such a relationship is only possible where there is a perfect and holy High Priest. This verse also implies that to be holy is to be like Jesus, *i.e.* harmless, undefiled, separate and (in the afterlife) utterly without sin. Just as Christians are called to suffer as Christ suffered,[16] so they are also called to be holy as Christ was holy. Admittedly, in this world no one can ever be perfectly holy but over a lifetime Christians should be moving in that direction. At the human level, holiness is to be equated with Christ-likeness.

Overall, **Hebrews 7:22-26** confirms that (like the Old Testament) the New Testament holds divine holiness in very high regard. The lofty standard (as laid down at Mount Sinai) remain in place with no diminution whatsoever from the Old to the New Testament. However, what has become clearer in the New Testament is how the Lawgiver of Sinai has also chosen to take on the role of gracious, compassionate Father. This role was made possible because of the holy priesthood of Jesus. Thanks to Christ's Priesthood, those believing in Him can dare to call God *'Father'* and boldly enter into the presence of a totally holy God and live. Permanent separation from God need no longer be a person's inevitable destiny.

Questions

1) List four characteristics of holiness. How does Christ's priesthood reconcile imperfect human beings with a totally perfect God?

2) How can Christ's priesthood help us know God as Father rather than as wrathful Judge?

3) Discuss the role of faith in making Christ's priesthood effective.

---

[16] However, unlike Christ they are not called to suffer by having the sins of the world placed upon them – this suffering were unique to Christ alone.

S3: God's Love and Divine Approachability in the Old Testament

The strong relationship existing between God's love and divine approachability is revealed throughout the Old Testament in a variety of ways: -

1) God's own character
Deuteronomy 4:37, 7:2-8 &13, 10:15, 23:5; 2 Chronicles 2:11; Isaiah 43:4, 63:9; Jeremiah 31:3; Hosea 11:1 & 4; Zephaniah 3:17 & Malachi 1:2

2) Divine compassion and pity
Exodus 20:6, 34:6; Deuteronomy 4:31; 2 Samuel 24:11; 2 Chronicles 30:9; Psalms 86:15, 103:8-13, 111:4, 119:156, 145:8; Isaiah 14:1, 49:13, 55:7, 60:10; Jeremiah 12:15, 30:18 & 31:20; Lamentations 3:22 & Micah 7:19

3) Divine grace (undeserved favour)
Genesis 30:27; Exodus 33:12 & 17, 34:9; Job 8:5, 19:11; Proverbs 3:34; Isaiah 9:14; Daniel 1:9, 4:22 & Zephaniah 3:17
4) Divine loving kindness
Psalms 17:7, 26:3, 36:7 & 10, 40:10-11, 42:8, 48:9, 51:1, 63:3, 69:16, 88:11, 89:33, 92:2, 103:4, 119:88, 149, 159, 138:2, 143:8; Jeremiah 9:24, 16:5, 31:3, 32:18 & Hosea 2:19

5) God's selection of Israel
Exodus 15:13 & 16, 19:4, 34:6-7; Deuteronomy 2:8, 8:14, 9:5 & 27, 10:14-15, 33:3; Isaiah 35:10, 42:21, 43:1-5, 15, 21, 54:5, 63:9; Jeremiah 3:4 & 19; 31:9 & 26; Ezekiel 16:1f & Hosea 11:1

Psalm 103:8-13 will be looked at in more depth. As in the previous section, a simple commentary will accompany each citation.

This Psalm was written by King David and is a celebration of divine forgiveness. David's intention was to *"Bless the Lord"* with all of his soul, and to remember *"all His benefits,"* (Psalm 103:1-2).

8. *"The Lord is merciful and gracious, slow to anger, and plentiful in mercy."*

After recalling how the Lord *"made known His ways unto Moses,"* David concentrates his thoughts upon God Himself. This time a very different aspect of His character is revealed from that of the inapproachable Lawgiver of Sinai. Here, David points out that God's anger is not easily provoked. Instead, God is viewed as being readily approachable and more than willing to show mercy to those who trust Him.

9. *"He will not always chide; neither will He keep His anger forever."*

In contrast to human anger, God's anger is always self-controlled. Although it can be very fierce, the Lord can and does curb it. If this were not so then the whole of Creation would already have been annihilated (totally destroyed) the moment the very first imperfection had appeared. God will, in future, remove all imperfection through the creation of *"a new heaven and a new earth,"* (Revelation 21:1). In the meantime, the only perfect way of dealing with the present flawed order of things has been (and continues to be) to follow a policy of gradual change. Through this strategy the *'long-suffering'* Lord shows that He wants all people to *"come to repentance."* (1 Peter 3:93) The fact that everything in the universe still exists provides testimony to the mercy of God. Without His compassion everything we now know will have ceased to have existed long ago.

10. *"He has dealt not with us after our sins, nor rewarded us according to our iniquities."*

If wrath is the expression of outraged holiness then mercy is the expression of gracious love. In the end, all of us will know either the fullness of divine wrath or divine mercy. The previous study of **Exodus 19:21f** has shown that divine wrath is neither avoided nor divine mercy earned by our own personal attempts to reach God. No matter how pious in their intent, religious devotions do not change this fact. Indeed, they serve only to increase human self-reliance, making us more fit to receive God's wrath rather than His mercy. This was precisely the danger that Jesus Himself warned against when challenging those who foolishly *"trusted in themselves,"* (Luke 18:9-14). Hell may well be crowded with religious people having been so busy trying to be pious that they'd completely overlooked the need to *'repent and believe.'* They'd failed to see that there's no such thing as salvation through piety. However, David did not make that mistake.

11. *"For as the heavens are far above the earth, so great is His mercy towards them who fear Him."*

Moving into poetical language, David infers that God's mercy can only be shown to those who fear Him. The word *'fear'* does <u>not</u> mean a cringing, paralysing panic, preventing all useful action. Rather, it is the very Hebrew concept of reverent awe. David was very aware of this respectful awe, which naturally led him to be single-minded and loyal to God. Ancient Hebrews, like David, respected God, both for who He was and for what He did. They believed in *'God Almighty,'* not *'God Almatey.'* Even today something of this reverence still exists in Orthodox Jewish communities throughout the World.

12. *"As far as the east is from the west, so far He has removed our transgressions from us."*

Forgiveness brings a tremendous sense of relief. <u>We are forgiven, not because we are good but because God is good.</u> More specifically, we are forgiven because Christ offered the supreme sacrifice to pacify God's perfectly justified outrage against sin. Even in David's day the Lord had Christ's future sacrifice in mind. It is this fact alone, which causes God to remove the sins of those who have trusted in Him. Yet even this element of trust is a gracious free gift from God. Without this God-given trust the barrier between an all-holy Lord and sinful rebellious humanity would still be firmly in place.

13. *"Like a father pities his children, so the Lord pities those who fear Him."*

Divine love leads to a constructive form of pity, which not only feels compassion for people but leads to practical measures promoting their welfare. His compassion is never forced upon anyone, but is quietly available to those who'd humbly receive it. (Those choosing to scorn the pity of God leave themselves with only the option of knowing His endless wrath.) The presence of this compassion explains why God the Father sent Jesus to die for our sins. To benefit from Christ's death a person must put a stop to trusting in their ability to please God and instead begin to trust in Jesus, believing He died to pacify God's justified fury against sin. Jesus is to be acknowledged as Saviour and believed in as Lord. Once this trust is in place the love of God begins its transforming work.[17]

---

[17] Should any reader feel unable to trust in Christ, then they should ask God to grant them the faith to do so; taking their model the prayer made in Mark 9:24c and cry *"Help me in my unbelief."*

Overall, **Psalm 103:8-13** demonstrates the main effect of divine love – to motivate the Lord to reach out to sinful humanity. People cannot ascend to God but God <u>chooses</u> to descend to people. He yearns to establish a relationship with those willing to trust His way of salvation. The picture of the frowning judge must be qualified by the picture of the pitying, gracious Father for both are of equal importance. Exactly how these apparently divergent qualities are reconciled will be discussed in Chapter 3.

Questions

1) Why does God allow people to approach Him even though they do not conform to His standards of absolute perfection?

2) Suggest how the Biblical picture of God as gracious Father can be reconciled with that of God as unapproachable Judge.

3) What role did Christ play in removing the barrier between God and humanity?

S4: God's Love and Divine Approachability in the New Testament

The strong relationship existing between God's love and divine approachability is revealed throughout the New Testament in a variety of ways: -

1) God's own character
Luke 11:42; John 3:16; Romans 5:5, 8:3-9; 2 Thessalonians 3:5; Titus 3:4; Jude :1; 1 John 2:5, 3:16-17, 4:8-9 & 5:3

2) God the Father and Son relationship within the Godhead
John 3:35, 5:20, 10:17, 14:31, 15:19 & 17:24-26

3) God-given salvation
Romans 9:23, 11:30; 1 Corinthians 7:25; 2 Corinthians 4:1; 1 Timothy 1:13 & Hebrews 4:16

4) Specific individuals
John 14:23, 16:27, 17:23; Romans 9:15 & Galatians 2:20

5) Specific sinners
Romans 2:4, 9:22; 1 Timothy 1:16 & 1 Peter 3:20

6) This world and the next
John 3:16, 15:10; Romans 5:7-8, 8:37; 1 John 4:9, 12 & Revelation 3:19

1 John 4:8-12 will now be looked at in more depth. A simple commentary will accompany each citation.

Having underlined the need to *"test the Spirits"* (1 John 4:1) the aged apostle is now stressing the importance of love in the Christian life. His intention is to protect the Church from the profanity caused by false teaching. He's aware that when God's love is present in the believer's life then the risk of spiritual deception is greatly reduced.

8. *"He that does not love does not know God; for God is love."*

All true teaching should promote love. If this love is not present then either the teaching is flawed or there has been a failure to apply it. By definition *'God is love.'* If something is not said or done in an attitude of love then it is not of God. Especially tragic are those situations where the word *'love'* is used to disguise its very absence. Because it is seen as something powerful within itself, *'love'* can be used to disguise malice. Sometimes the foulest of accusations are made in the name of *'love'* and those who say; *'May I say this in love...'* are probably best viewed with suspicion – for when such words are spoken, *'love'* is usually not at the heart of the matter! Proverbs 18:24a does warn about those *"who only pretend to be friends."*

The love of God is radically different from this false human love – not least because it always has the genuine welfare of true believers at heart. The whole concept of divine love means that God is also: -
- Charitable[18]
- Compassionate
- Merciful
- Reasonable
- Self-giving
- Tender
- Warm-hearted

---

[18] Today the words *'charity'* or *'charitable'* conjure up the mental image of a charity shop, but here, it refers to the active outworking and positive application of divine love in other people's lives.

This list could be increased to infinity, and even then the depths of divine love will not have been exhausted.

9. *"In this was manifested the love of God towards us, because God sent His only begotten Son into the world, that we might live through Him."*

God's love has been supremely demonstrated in Jesus Christ whose example showed that where love is present, there is fullness of life. However, this divine love is not bestowed upon everyone in equal measure. A greater concentration is given to those who believe in Christ. As a result, their sins are restrained and they are far more able to love God and their fellow human beings. This Christian love is <u>not</u> generated by human self-effort but is completely God-given. Furthermore, divine love also acts as the link between God and His ability to beget a Son. Without a Son, God would remain as a remote lawgiver whose displays of compassion would be totally arbitrary. He would be like an eastern despot showing mercy only when He felt like it. Happily, the eternal relationship He has enjoyed with His Son has motivated the Father to fully manifest His love toward those sinners for whom His Son died. The Father loves us because of His Son who, as our *'Great High Priest,'* constantly intercedes on our behalf.

10. *"Herein is love, <u>not</u> that we loved God, but that He loved us and sent His Son to be the propitiation for our sins."*

The supreme demonstration of divine love was the death of Christ. The word *'propitiation'* means the complete pacification of God's holy and justified outrage against sin.[19] Christ Himself has pacified God's holy wrath so that He no longer finds our presence to be a mortal offence. At the cross both the requirements of holiness and love were perfectly satisfied. <u>Thanks to Christ's sacrificial death, God is no longer unapproachable.</u> He is very willing to share His love with those who have put their trust in His Son, Jesus. We could never hope to love God without Christ – we simply do <u>not</u> have the innate capacity to love Him in a way that is acceptable to His holiness. As God the Father loves us <u>through</u> Christ, so we can only approach and love God <u>through</u> Christ too.

11. *"Beloved, if God so loved us, we also ought to love one another."*

---

[19] Orthodox Jewish communities still carry this sense of awe during their Synagogue Liturgies, even though they don't believe in Jesus.

When divine love is present in the believer's life it must inevitably spill over to bless others. Exactly how this happens will vary, but there is no such thing as a true love hoarding its blessings all to itself. By nature, the love of God is *'other person'* centred. One effect of such compassion is to cure self-pity; when meeting the needs of others we forget our own problems.

12. *"No man has seen God at any time. If we love one another, God dwells in us and His love is perfected* [matured] *in us."*

God does not always have to be seen through some form of dramatic revelation. He can be seen in the small things of life *e.g.* through the commonplace favours people show to one another and through the provision of life's basic necessities. Indeed, the effect of love should be to wean us away from any unhealthy hankering after supernatural experiences. It must also be emphasised that growing in love is a lifelong process wherein no exact point is ever reached when we can claim to have gained perfect love. The virtue of compassionate love needs to ripen over time, through much patient nurturing and continual submission to God's will (once this has been clearly discerned).

Overall, **1 John 4:8-12** shows the centrality of love in the Christian life. God does not keep His love to Himself – He shares it and expects us to share it too. Divine love is not to be idolised and isolated solely as an object of private contemplation; rather, it is to be practised amidst the full rigours of daily life. This is possible only through the indwelling of God's precious Holy Spirit. We're able to love only because He first loved us.

From this section it is possible to conclude that: -

1) Both the Old and New Testaments employ a variety of literary forms to reveal the divine attributes of holiness and love. Consequently, it would be mistaken to allege that either Testament concentrates upon one attribute at the expense of the other. However, it is reasonable to suggest that both attributes are revealed more fully in the New rather than the Old Testament.
2) Divine holiness and love act in unison and not in opposition to one another. They co-exist harmoniously with all of the other divine attributes, thanks in part to God's almighty power.

Questions

1) List seven characteristics of divine love.

2) How did Christ's death satisfy the requirements of holiness and love?

3) What problems are likely to restrict a believer's growth in love? Suggest ways to alleviate such problems.

S5: Deviant Forms of Christianity

Having looked closely at both divine holiness and divine love the next step is to highlight the need to keep both in equal focus. To err in this would lead to an imbalance in the Christian life. At this point, *'The Denial Method'* may be used to ask, *'what are the likely logical and practical consequences of denying*: -
1) *The existence of divine holiness?*
2) *The existence of divine love?*
3) *The unity of divine holiness and divine love?'*
Underlying *'The Denial Method'* is the assumption, that over time, intellectual muddle leads inexorably to practical muddle. The intellectual and practical areas cannot be separated.

To deny or overlook the existence of divine holiness leads to a casual disregard of Biblical teaching. Nowhere is this truer than in Western Christianity where whole networks of Churches have surrendered to the values of a decadent society. As Biblical words have become stripped of their meaning, it has become all too easy to overlook teachings on unpleasant matters like hell or judgement. Moreover, where divine holiness is assumed to be incompatible with divine love it becomes far easier to focus only upon God's love. Other attributes like divine wrath are ignored and may not receive even a token mention in sermons. Hence, *'The Denial Method'* shows that the *'Oppositionist model'* creates the problem of *'attribute misfocus.'* In addition, where love is emphasised at the expense of holiness *'a religion of flippancy'* has tended to emerge, often with the following characteristics: -
1) A lack of resilience in the face of hardship and persecution
2) An *'outward form of religion,'* minus the power
3) A pragmatic *'if it works, let's do it'* mentality
4) A very lax *'anything goes'* attitude toward morality
5) An artificial *'niceness'* – which refuses to confront important issues

6) An indifferent attitude toward doctrinal matters
7) Bland, ineffectual preaching at the one extreme and emotional manipulation at the other
8) Lack of internal discipline, sins are either *'hushed up'* or excused
9) A lust for novelty, often accompanied by a desire to be *'trendy'* and up to date
10) A craving for sensationalism and religious melodrama
11) A desire for unity based upon common experience rather than shared belief
12) Poor organisational and administrative structures
13) A lack of spiritual discipline, *e.g.* Bible reading and prayer are despised or ignored
14) A widespread slothful, superficiality

On moral matters, worldly attitudes most often prevail; entertainment is used as a substitute for worship; doctrinal error may be tolerated or even encouraged; false teachers and prophets are openly welcomed despite the harm they inflict upon vulnerable people.

Upon careful reflection, it simply does not pay to neglect divine holiness. The long-term result is a flabby, weak Christianity that has no doctrinal grounding or moral authority. Tragically, this is precisely the form of Christianity now prevailing within both the United Kingdom and the United States. Furthermore, when evidence of divine displeasure has clearly begun to be seen people have become *'locked in denial,'* totally relying upon the view that, *'God is our loving Father, we are His children; He won't judge us, we are the King's kids.'*[20] All that preachers can offer is platitudinous waffle about how *'God loves us just as we are.'*

Lying further ahead is the possibility that today's *'all you need is love'* Christianity will open the Church up to a series of deceptions far more terrible than the Toronto debacle. This is because people will have been lulled into a false sense of complacency (after all, God loves them – with all that that entails – He will take care of them no matter what). Apostles like Paul warned against just such a complacency, (1 Corinthians 10:12).[21]

---

[20] The writer personally saw how this kind of stance reached ridiculous proportions during the Toronto Deception of 1994-1997.
[21] With hindsight, one of the most striking features of the Toronto deception was the way in which so many Christian leaders thought it impossible that they could fall into error. Quite subconsciously, they seemed to follow a bizarre kind of reasoning, which stated, *'Because God is love, He will not allow me to be deceived by Satan, therefore any voice or revelation that comes into my head is of divine origin.'* Despite his

If anything, the Toronto Deception served only to reinforce this unbalanced emphasis upon love.[22] Tragically, this form of sub-scriptural reasoning makes it impossible for people to remain aware of any impending danger. Taking the absurdly superficial view that *'God accepts me as I am'* serves only to negate the very notion of repentance. Those believing it have let down their guard and are in the naively credulous mindset which thinks that anything said and done *'in the name of love'* must be perfectly acceptable. It follows that, should the anti-Christ emerge such people will be amongst the first to follow him. In the English-speaking world, most churches are ripe for deception – it's not so much a question of *'if'* but *'when'* this will happen. This is simply because of their drift away from a firm scriptural base. When it comes to matters of faith and morality many professing Christians prefer to *'make things up as they go along.'* Any arguments they put forward will simply reflect the cultural prejudices of their day.

However, evil consequences can also arise when divine love is neglected. Where holiness is emphasised at the expense of love the most likely consequence is a growing sense of God's absence which breeds *'a religion of fear.'* This in turn produces the following characteristics: -
1) Self-inflicted hardship and mortification
2) An over-emphasis upon the keeping of outward religious forms and ceremonies
3) A petty-minded rigidity over minor matters
4) A legalistic *'even sex in marriage is dirty'* attitude toward morality
5) An intransigent harshness (and sometimes bitterness of spirit) – frequently leading to unnecessary confrontations over peripheral matters

---

renunciation of Pentecostalism in December 1997, the writer is the last person on earth to deny that God can speak directly <u>when He so chooses.</u> However, such forms of communication should be rigorously tested with all of the thoroughness of a scientific experiment. What the aforementioned leaders failed to realise was that God could actually use false prophets to test the loyalty of His people (a point highlighted in Deuteronomy 12:3). The overemphasis upon divine love had led those leaders to the incorrect assumption that they were immune from error. When the writer made any attempt to challenge this assumption the response was often either furious rage or an evasive furtiveness. Hate mail was another response. Other Christians (including elderly ladies) who also challenged this error met with a similar response.

[22] Any form of Christianity, which tolerates animal noises, convulsive twitching and people standing on their head (in order to prove *'the world had been turned upside down'*), has long since lost sight of divine holiness and has become ripe for judgement.

6) A fanatical attitude in relation to doctrinal matters
7) Polemical (often hate-filled) preaching, used in order to bludgeon an audience into submission
8) Rigid discipline and control – with frequent punitive punishments of perceived dissenters
9) A reactionary *'clinging onto dead human traditions'* for reasons of emotional security
10) A morbid distrust of anything to do with the arts or culture; the worldly pursuits and pleasures are seen as something to be shunned
11) Exclusivity and a tendency to be isolated from others who are not *'like-minded.'*
12) Hierarchical organisational structures with clear chains of command
13) Excessive religiosity, characterised by over-frequent meetings, over-long sermons and in extreme cases, systematic sleep deprivation
14) A sour and widespread hypocrisy leading to a covering-up of abuses

On moral matters, a world-hating attitude more often prevails. Dreary repetition and dirge-like hymns are often used as a substitute for worship. There may be persecution and the murder of perceived dissenters as was the case with the Spanish Inquisition. Such consequences arise because when people feel that God is uncaring they tend to adopt an uncaring attitude toward others. They may also suffer from feelings of resentment that only find release when some convenient scapegoat is targeted. All this shows that where religious faith lacks any sense of divine love it turns people into neurotics. Present is an edgy frustration that can erupt into overt acts of violence. This explains why great piety is often associated with great cruelty. Evidence for this point could be drawn from every world religion. Paradoxically, a strong religious faith can be the most liberating and enslaving of qualities.

Upon careful reflection, it clearly does not pay to neglect divine love; to do so results in a harsh, legalistic Christianity, which <u>exceeds</u> the doctrinal basis of scripture. Tragically, this is precisely the form of Christianity now prevalent in the Eastern Orthodox Church of the former Soviet Union. Furthermore, when evidence of divine displeasure is present people have again locked themselves in denial, taking the stance that *'We are the one True Holy Church, possessing the Creeds, the Fathers and the holy Icons of the saints; God won't judge us.'* (However, being given over to Islam and

Communism immediately refutes this stance.) Indeed, Eastern Orthodoxy as a whole bears some resemblance to the Church of Pergamum in Revelation 2:12-16. This Church had doggedly clung onto the faith even under pressure from Caesar worship. (It also had a faithful martyr called Antipas) and yet it had succumbed to the idolatries of Balaam (*i.e.* Icon veneration) and to the falsehood of the Nicolaitians (*i.e.* the adoption of Greek Philosophy and hierarchical forms of organization). Christ's response to such developments was to warn; *"I ... will fight against them with the sword of my mouth,"* (Revelation 3:16b). In the case of Pergamum, *'the sword'* represented the teachings of scripture, but for Eastern Orthodoxy as a whole it came to represent *'the swords'* of Islam and Communism.

My own experience of the Eastern Orthodox Tradition is meagre. However, near the end of 1991, I did contact a certain Eastern Orthodox Priest by telephone, requesting to see their liturgy at first-hand. Being Greek Cypriot, this man's English was poor and for some reason he believed I was a Roman Catholic. The result was a tirade of self-righteous indignation, which raked up all that the Catholics had done at the siege of Constantinople in 1204. Sensing the man was beyond reason, I waited until he had finished. Then, on the Sunday before Christmas 1991 I had cause to be in his inner city locality and called into his Church. I was greeted by a little wizened priest, small in stature with a thin grey beard and a very sour facial expression. After I quoted the Church Fathers to put him more at ease he deigned to allow him to sit through their Judaeo-Gnostic liturgy (fixed order of service).[23] Providentially, the priest concerned did not appear to identify me with the man who'd telephoned him earlier.

What the above real-life example shows is that impressive ritual doesn't compensate for a lack of love or elementary courtesy. More ominously, where there is an obvious lack of divine holiness or divine love repentance may become impossible. Where love is emphasised and holiness is ignored people become too complacent to repent; and where holiness is emphasised and love is overlooked people

---

[23] The Judaic element conveyed a sense of awe and respect for God. In contrast, the Gnostic element seemed only to venerate Ancient Egyptian funerary portraits (called Icons) some of which contained pictures of Angels, (paying homage to Angels was a very Gnostic custom.) Briefly, what was best in Greek Orthodox Liturgy derived from Judaism and what was worst came from a mixture of Gnosticism and Ancient Roman Emperor worship.

become too self-righteous to repent. Maintaining a balance between these two attributes can be essential to spiritual survival.

With regard to, *'the likely consequences of denying the unity of divine holiness and divine love?'* it's clear that all that would remain is the view that God as in impersonal creative *'force'* the essence of which is totally unknowable. All we could do is lapse into a *'Star Wars'* theology with its spurious blessing *'May the force be with you.'*[24] The obvious outcome of this line of reasoning is to question the need to bother with such an *'unknowable'* deity in the first place. To all intents and purposes people may as well live as if God did not exist at all.

Another likely consequence of denying the unity of divine holiness and divine love is the view that God is a *'split personality'* whose holiness is constantly at war with His love. Seen in this light, the death of Jesus did not represent a demonstration of the already existing perfect unity between these two attributes; but instead was a panic driven expedient designed to reconcile two bitterly opposed attributes. From a historical perspective, divine holiness and love were once viewed as being so hostile to one another that certain outlandish second century spiritual deceptions such as Marcionism[25] suggested each opposed attribute was attached to two separate Gods! Hence *'holiness'* tended to be equated with the *'inferior God!'* of the Old Testament, whereas *'love'* was equated with the *'superior God'* of the New. Like many errors, Marcionism suffered from a certain smallness of mind. It failed to see that <u>one perfect God was fully capable of manifesting both holiness and love.</u> A variation of this error was to associate one member of the Trinity with holiness and another with love. Hence, the Father was exclusively associated with holiness and the Son with love. A picture emerges of a wrathful Jehovah who was only restrained from hurtling His thunderbolts because of the tearful appeals of His Son, Jesus (or in some versions His mother, the Virgin Mary).The fact is that <u>all three members of the Trinity possess an infinite degree of holiness and an infinite degree of love.</u> Perhaps even more dangerous is the view of the Trinity as a lofty, abstract entity, fit only for obtuse philosophical speculation.

---

[24] *'Star Wars'* consisted of a series of six very popular Science Fiction films, released during the period of 1977-2005. The writer has seen some of them.
[25] The early Church Father Tertullian displayed great enthusiasm in refuting Marcion's views.

All the above would confirm that any denial of the essential unity between divine holiness and divine love leads only to incorrect views of God. Moreover, such incorrect views can distort worship and lead to a situation where imaginary mediators are relied upon in place of Christ. To make God appear more real and accessible the Virgin Mary has often become the human embodiment of divine love and it is her tears rather than Christ's, which are seen as being responsible for pacifying the Father's wrath.

At this point, it is worth stressing that any particular view of God will eventually produce consequences affecting every area of life. Whether these consequences are good or bad will depend upon how true to scripture a particular view of God really is. Certainly, viewing Him as some form of *'split personality'* is most unlikely to produce good results, (because He will have been viewed as being inconsistent and therefore untrustworthy). The *'oppositionist model'* simply encourages a negative view of God. Should the believer (even unwittingly) adopt this model then he or she is left with the overriding impression that active strife exists <u>between</u> and <u>within</u> the members of the Trinity. Again such a *'split personality'* view of God does little to engender confidence in Him. This model, by its own inherent nature, denies divine perfection – a God who is not perfect is simply not God in any meaningful sense of the word. All that remains is a cosmic neurotic, more to be pitied than praised. Undeniably, over recent decades, the assumed schism (hostile division) between divine holiness and love has fostered a complacent irresponsibility and taken the *'bite'* out of much of contemporary preaching. This has often degenerated into a vague *'God loves you always'* sentimentality, with His holiness being ignored completely. Christians have also become prone to deceptive spiritual influences simply because the Holy Spirit, grieved by the incorrect notions held about God, has reduced the level of protection He provides.

Adhering to the *'oppositionist model'* causes God to be fashioned into the impersonal *'it'* of the New Age Movement. Any attempt to overlook this vital relationship (of divine holiness and love) causes the Biblical view of God to unravel. Strip holiness from love and the result is a jovial *'Santa-Claus God'* who can never say *'no'* to the most childish of human whims. Conversely, strip love from holiness and all that remains is a wrathful Jehovah, hurtling out thunderbolts for the slightest misdemeanour. Both forms of *'attribute misfocus,'* create a distorted view of God, each veering wildly away from the teaching of scripture. Divine perfection is denied, so that whatever is being followed and believed in is simply not God at all or certainly not the God of scripture.

Such problems indicate that the *'oppositionist model'* run counter to the interlocking nature of Christian doctrine. Denial of one important Biblical teaching leads inexorably to a denial of other important Biblical teachings. True Biblical faith is lost – swamped by humanistic, moralistic teaching. Should the link between God's holiness and love be broken, a severance of the links between all of the other divine attributes results, with the correct Bible-based view of God being drowned in a morass of confusion. Any positive outworking which may once have stemmed from believing in these attributes becomes muted or even lost altogether. *'The Denial Method'* shows that it simply does not pay to separate divine holiness from divine love – to do so only reinforces a move toward apostasy.

From this section it is possible to conclude that: -

1) To neglect any divine attribute produces only bitter consequences; repentance itself is made very difficult

2) Neglecting both attributes of holiness and love reduces God to an impersonal creative *'force'* with little relevance to daily living

3) Both scripture and common sense support the *'Essentialist'* rather than the *'Oppositionist'* model of divine holiness and love.

4) The death of Jesus demonstrated the already existing unity between divine holiness and love; <u>it was definitely not a case of Jesus having to die to reconcile two opposing attributes</u>

5) The *'oppositionist model'* fails because: -
5.1 It does not adhere to the correct Biblical view of God
5.2 It tends to place one attribute above another
5.3 It fails to see that the attributes of holiness and love are inextricably intertwined
5.4 It underestimates the power of God to preserve the essential unity between divine holiness and love
5.5 It leads to an unworthy view of God as a *'split personality'*

5.6 It leads to *'attribute misfocus,'* where one attribute is accepted at the expense of another

5.7 It runs contrary to the interlocking nature of Christian doctrine

Questions

1) What problems may arise when God's holiness is separated from His love?

2) Suggest how a balanced view of divine holiness and love can be maintained.

3) How can a balanced view of divine holiness and love help people to repent of their sins?

C2:

Midrash Bible Expositions

S1: Homiletic Midrash

This Midrash Bible Exposition focuses upon <u>the uniqueness of the one true God, who simultaneously possesses both unlimited holiness and unlimited love.</u> As scripture states: -

Genesis 18:14
"Is anything too hard for the Lord?"

Exodus 20:3
"You shall have no other Gods but me."

Joshua 24:19
"And Joshua said unto the people, 'you cannot serve the Lord; for He is a Holy God: He is a jealous God; He will not forgive your transgressions or your sins."

Job 40:2
"Shall He that contends with the Almighty instruct Him? He that rebukes God let him answer it."

Isaiah 63:9
"In all their [Israel's] affliction He was afflicted, and the Angel of His presence saved them. In His love and His pity He redeemed them, and carried them all the days of old."

Zephaniah 3:17
"The Lord your God in the midst of you is mighty. He will save, He will rejoice over you with joy, He will rest in His love, He will rejoice over you with singing."

Mark 10:18
"There is none good but one, that is God."

John 4:24
"God is Spirit; and they who worship Him [must] worship Him in spirit and in truth."

Romans 5:5
"Our hope is not shameful because the love of God is shed abroad in our hearts by the Holy Spirit who is given to us."

1 John 4:8
"He that does not love does not know God; for God is love."

Jude 21
"Keep yourselves in the love of God, looking for the mercy of our Lord Jesus Christ unto eternal life."

Revelation 4:8
"And the four [Angelic] beasts had each of them six wings about him and they were full of eyes within, and they rest not day and night, saying, 'Holy, Holy, Holy, Lord God Almighty, who was, and is and is to come.'"

1) From the six <u>Old Covenant</u> Bible passages it is possible to discover that: -
1.1 Nothing is too hard for God
1.2 The one true God forbids the worship of all other gods
1.3 Divine holiness motivates God's jealousy, which then leads to punishment of sin
1.4 God lies beyond the reach of any human rebuke
1.5 Divine love motivates God to redeem ruined sinners
1.6 Divine power enables God to rescue people from evil

2) From the six <u>New Covenant</u> Bible passages it is possible to discover that: -
2.1 Divine holiness is expressed in the goodness of God
2.2 God is a spiritual being who inspires people to worship Him
2.3 Divine love is manifested through the Holy Spirit's work in the human heart
2.4 By definition, God is love
2.5 People have a responsibility to remain in God's love
2.6 The highest-ranking angels in heaven celebrate divine holiness

From this section, it is possible to conclude that the close relationship between God's holiness and love can help account for His apparently simultaneous inapproachability and approachability. He is well able to enjoy apparently contradictory attributes. For every reader, the challenge remains to discover the means whereby God can be made approachable through the forgiveness of sins. Hope can be drawn from some of the encouragements given in the previously quoted extracts.

Questions

1) Which of the twelve quoted passages mentions divine holiness and which divine love?

2) To what extent do you agree (or disagree) with the view which states, 'The Old Testament reveals God's holiness and the New Testament reveals His love.' Give reasons for your answer.

S2: Parashiyot Midrash

The main theme of this Midrash is the way in which God's almighty power forges an underlying unity between divine holiness and love.[26] To provide evidence for this point Psalm 99:9, Isaiah 63:9a and Jeremiah 32:7 will be examined.

Psalm 99:9
"Exalt the Lord our God and worship at His holy hill [the Temple Mount]; *for the Lord our God is Holy."*

This Psalm represents a call to worship God on the Temple Mount at Jerusalem and the reason for such worship is that *'the Lord our God is holy.'* These words form a clear doctrinal statement, either to be believed in or not. God is either holy or He is not holy. Also apparent in these words is the implication that a high view of God encourages a reverent and exultant worship. Implicit in them is the view that God is the Almighty King, reigning over every aspect of His Creation. However, if seen in isolation from the wider teaching of scripture this verse could create the impression that God is a lofty and remote figure. An unbridgeable gulf is perceived to exist between God and humanity.

---

[26] Here it's worth reminding the reader that in a typical Parashiyot structure a base text (known as a Petkah) is followed by an apparently conflicting text; a final reconciling text then follows. Each text has a brief comment, focussing upon key points. A Parashiyot Midrash is a very traditional Jewish method of handling apparent discrepancies within a sacred text.

Isaiah 63:9a
"In their affliction He was afflicted, and the angel of His presence saved them. In His love and in His pity He redeemed them."

In this text, the prophet obviously has the Israelites' deliverance from Egypt in mind. As verse 10 indicates, his intention is to contrast divine faithfulness with human disloyalty. This verse also contains a clear doctrinal statement which again either has to be believed in or not; God is either a God of love or He is not a God of love. It also implies that this attribute of love is associated with overriding feelings of pity, the fullest depths of which cannot be fully appreciated on this side of eternity. However, their very presence excludes the notion, (common throughout Greek philosophy) that God is an impassable Being – having no emotional feelings toward His Creation. Such a philosophy represents the teaching of Plato rather than divine revelation.[27] Returning to the verse in hand, if it is seen in isolation from the wider teaching of scripture it could create the impression that God is not excessively worried by the presence of sin in His people. No gulf is seen to exist between God and the human race, thus allowing people to continue unchallenged in their sin.

Jeremiah 32:27
"Behold, I am the Lord, the God of all flesh. Is there anything too hard for me?"

Here, God was warning Jeremiah that Jerusalem will be given over *"to the hands of the Chaldeans and of their King, Nebuchadnezzar,"* (V28). Of particular interest is the rhetorical question *"Is there anything too hard for me?"* The wording implies that it is certainly <u>not too hard for God to hold together His divine holiness and love through the exercise of His almighty power.</u> Without the slightest exertion, He holds together, <u>in perfect unity,</u> both these and all of the other attributes. Only a *'phantom conflict'* exists between them. In God there exists a Shalom[28] Echad (a peaceful and flawlessly complete, if complex, unity) between all of the infinite number of His attributes. Fallible, weak human beings may find it difficult to hold together such qualities as holiness and love but this is certainly <u>not</u> the case with God for whom all things are possible.

---

[27] This view was largely brought into the Church by some of the Church Fathers – most notably Augustine of Hippo.
[28] The Hebrew word *'Shalom'* means *'peace'* and also has definite connotations with personal completeness and wholeness.

During times of affliction we may be comforted by the thought that God can deliver us from our suffering or provide as with the strength to endure it. For as Saint Paul promised in 1 Corinthians 10:13, God will not allow us to be tested beyond our endurance. In response to His holy love, we are not to give up the faith in times of adversity or persecution. We can also trust that God will resolve any conflicting emotions we may feel at such times. So let us go on and persevere in our relationship with Him.

From this Section, it's possible to conclude that: -

1) God's unlimited and almighty power unifies divine holiness and divine love, with no degree of friction

2) A flawless unity exists between all of God's divine attributes

3) People may still find it difficult to grasp how a perfect unity exists between all of these divine attributes

4) Christians are to draw comfort and strength from God's unlimited power

Questions

1) How can a Parashiyot Midrash reconcile seemingly contradictory passages of scripture?

2) What are the limitations of Parashiyot Midrash Bible Interpretation?

3) Using any of the previous Bible references in this book construct another Parashiyot Midrash to illustrate the unity between divine holiness and love.

S3: Peshar Midrash

In **Revelation 4:8** God's Word states:
"And the four beasts
[High ranking Seraphim or Angelic Beings]
Had each of them six wings about them
And they were full of eyes
And they rest not day or night, saying,
 'Holy, Holy, Holy,
Lord God Almighty,
Who was, and is and is to come."

Having delivered prophetic messages to seven Churches, John the writer, has just been granted a dramatic vision of heavenly worship to encourage him during his time of exile on the island of Patmos. In an attempt to describe the indescribable he draws upon Old Testament images and words, depicting some of the distressing events *"which must be hereafter,"* (Revelation 4:13). Both the content and style of the Book of Revelation show that John viewed his own role as being akin to that of the Old Testament Prophets.

Revelation 4:8 shows that God is praised for being holy, sovereign, perfect, almighty, eternal, glorious and omnipresent – in short, God is celebrated for being God. His presence fills even the highest-ranking angels with awe. Of particular interest is the fact that all of these attributes are seen as being coexistent, with <u>no</u> hint of internal conflict; this graphically represents the essential unity of God.[29] In addition, the sheer enthusiasm with which God is praised by these angelic beings confirms their profound love for Him.[30]

The same point can be made concerning Isaiah's vision, which commissioned him to be a prophet to the stubborn people of Judah (Isaiah 6:1f). He too saw the seraphim, which were so awe-struck that, despite their mighty power, they covered their faces with their wings. God was so utterly great in His holiness that even the seraphim would have found Him unapproachable were it not for His

---

[29] Possibly present are faint echoes of Trinitarian doctrine wherein the Father, Son and Holy Spirit are viewed as the three *'holies'* of God. However, this is <u>not</u> a passage which could be used as a key text to establish Trinitarian teaching. This is because its focus is far more upon God's essential rather than His personal unity. To establish the doctrine of the Trinity other more relevant texts would need to be consulted.

[30] In passing, it's worth noting that an exuberant form of praise often expresses a passionately felt love.

mercy. In Verse 3, they *"cried to one another saying, 'Holy holy, holy is the Lord of* [angelic] *Hosts; the whole earth is full of His glory."* The implication here is that God's glory is not confined to the heavens – it also covers *'the whole earth.'*

Isaiah's reaction to this manifestation of divine holiness is interesting. He exclaims in verse 5, *"Woe is me! I am undone, because I am a man of unclean lips, and I dwell in the midst of a people of unclean lips; for my eyes have seen the King, the Lord of Hosts."* This direct encounter with the divine has aroused in Isaiah a feeling of total unworthiness. <u>His experience is shown to be true because it has humbled him and brought him face to face with the awfulness of his own sin.</u> By the standards of the time Isaiah was a good man. However, when compared to the perfect standards of God he was like everyone else – a sinner ripe for judgement. This sense of divine holiness is precisely what is missing in many Churches today – especially those that claim to be *'Spirit led.'* During January 1995, in one supposed Christian centre in the North of England a certain church leader had twitched and doubled up like an epileptic whilst boasting to his audience, *'Huh, huh, it's catching.'* This silly man had also the impertinence to claim that he was under the anointing of the Holy Spirit. Yet it was precisely the sense of God's utter holiness that was totally missing. This spirit was shown to be false by its abject frivolity.[31]

In Isaiah's case, his experience led him to move directly from a position of condemnation to one of redemption. In verses 6-7 one of the seraphim was sent to announce; *"Your iniquity is taken away and your sin is purged,"* (Isaiah 6:7c). Only then was Isaiah ready to accept God's calling to be a prophet. There appears to be a pattern wherein a revelation from God leads firstly, to a sense of total personal or corporate unworthiness; secondly, to a sense of joy at divine forgiveness and thirdly, to a calling to perform a particular task, (which, under normal circumstances could never be undertaken upon natural human strength alone.) Sometimes, the order of this sequence may vary but all three elements need to be present if an experience of God is to be valid. However, in some cases these elements may be spread over a number of occasions because weak human beings may not be capable of handling everything at once.

---

[31] This detail is based upon a first-hand account by a source close to the author. Subsequent video evidence showed that he also displayed the infamous *'Toronto twitch'* (a hypnotic reaction causing people to double over, often accompanied by groaning and moaning sounds).

Hints of this three-fold pattern emerge in Ezekiel 1-2, (which also contains a vision of God surrounded by worshipping angelic Beings). Along with Isaiah and John in Revelation, Ezekiel experienced a feeling of being completely overwhelmed. Relief was provided in the form of comforting words and an empowering of divine strength for a calling to fulfil a naturally impossible task. Ezekiel 2:1, which contains the command, *"Son of Man, stand on your feet and I will speak to you,"* is of special interest. It implies that God will usually speak to people only after they are standing firmly upon their feet and able to use their minds to listen to Him. Along with Revelation 1:17-19, this verse from Ezekiel shows that, if people do fall down as an emotional response to a manifestation of divine power, then God soon wants them back upon their feet again, engaging in intelligent dialogue. There is no hint of God *'pinning'* people to the floor, unable to move for hours at a time. Such a phenomenon has more to do with either stage hypnosis or even demonic activity. In contrast, when God moves in grace, His Holy Spirit always respects the dignity of human beings — He does not make a foolish spectacle of them. As 2 Timothy 1:7 asserts, *"God has not given us the Spirit of fear; but of power, and of love and of a sound mind."* This quotation confirms the personalising effect of divine power.[32] When God moves in spiritual power to bless people, He always increases those attributes which make them more human. The will is enlarged, the mind quickened and the emotions purified. In addition, a person's ability to relate effectively to others is improved. People become more who they should be in Christ, with the godly aspects of their individual identities strengthened. Doctrinal orthodoxy is also given its proper place. What God does not do (except possibly by way of a very severe judgement) is to obliterate the human personality. Respecting the dignity of His Creation, He does not turn people into laughing maniacs or passive zombies. Should such occurrences take place within the Church it is a sure sign of judgement. As a punishment for long-standing faithlessness on the part of Christians the Lord pours out, *"the spirit of deep sleep,"* (Isaiah 29:10a); mistaking such judgement as blessing has been one of the tragedies of this present Age.

---

[32] Augustine, in some of his anti-Pelagic writings, stressed that one effect of God's work upon a person is an enlargement of the human will, (pp 456-7 of his treatise on *'Grace and freewill'*). This *'personalising effect of divine power'* also has implications for the whole issue of election. If an exercise of divine power does not cause people to be more human than it is difficult to see how there could ever be any scope for freedom of will or a sense of personal responsibility.

In my own case, the three previously mentioned elements were spread over a number of powerful experiences. Around 8.00pm on the evening of Saturday 18th October 1975 there was the element of joy when I was converted through a vision of Christ. This occurred at a small Christian Union Meeting with only three others were present. This note of joy continued through my Baptism of the Holy Spirit at 9:28pm[33] on Thursday 27th November 1975; a very gentle experience. Almost a year later, following a disastrous summer trying to do Social Work in London,[34] I was almost crushed by the weight of my own sinfulness (around 3.00pm on Friday, 22nd October 1976). However, it was only from the late 1985 to 1990 period that God used a variety of media to call me into a teaching ministry, which was to be instrumental in diverting significant numbers of people from the Toronto Deception.[35] Indeed, I quickly saw the spurious nature of this experience in July 1994, partly because it had nothing at all in common with the way the Lord had dealt with me over the previous two decades. Far more importantly, the Toronto Deception diverged from scripture in both its manifestations and its doctrinal content. However, when this was pointed out to various recipients of this so called *'blessing'* their reaction was often one of anger, evasion or mute incomprehension; their experience having robbed them of their own ability to reason things for themselves. In some cases, the symptoms were akin to those unfortunate suffered a stroke.[36]

Previously cited passages confirm that, <u>what really matters is not whether a particular religious experience has spectacular manifestations, but whether its content is based upon scripture.</u> If an experience does **not** lead people to follow the God revealed in **Revelation 4:8** then it is to be rejected. Experience by itself tells nothing; <u>it is the doctrinal content of the experience which is all-important.</u> Incidentally, this was a point that Moses emphasised in

---

[33] The writer just happened to glance at a wall clock during this time.
[34] This was from Friday, July 16th until Friday, August 28th 1976 during a blazing hot summer.
[35] It was also instrumental in causing him to challenge certain parties in Anglicanism about the neo-pagan deceptions associated with Archbishop Rowan Williams (July 2004-August 2008).
[36] This was most clearly seen in February 1996 during a direct verbal confrontation with two of the Church leaders who had tried to *'push'* the Toronto Experience onto their congregation. One man looked as though he was desperately trying to grasp something he couldn't quite remember. His physical features reminded the writer of stroke patients he had seen when engaged in hospital visiting (from the January 1985 to September 1995). Incidentally, both the writer and contacts he knew, noticed how this pattern of confusion was frequently displayed by those who had succumbed to this deception.

Deuteronomy 13:1-5, when he showed the Israelites how to distinguish a true from a false prophet. Always, when dealing with an experience a person should ask *'What does it say about God and His teachings in the Bible?'* When God speaks He expects us to use our minds in an intelligent, thoughtful way. Lending weight to this view is God's own exhortation in Isaiah 1:18, which states; *"Come, let us reason together says the Lord, although your sins be as scarlet, they shall be as white as snow; although they be red like crimson, they shall be white as wool."* Also, in their own prayers and encounters with God, both Jesus and the Apostles were called to use their minds (reasoning faculties). There was no question of them having to empty their minds in order to receive some experience of *'divine light.'*

Markedly different in spirit is the advice of Dionysius the Aereopagite (who appears to have been a Syrian monk, writing under an assumed name in around 500AD). He counselled that *"in the earnest exercise of mystic contemplation"* one *"should leave the senses and the activities of the intellect."* Only after one has laid one's *"understanding to rest"* would it then be possible to *"strain as far as you can toward a Union with him"* who is God.[37] From this teaching one would almost have thought that Isaiah 1:18 had said, *"Come switch off your minds in order to ascend through contemplation to a mystical union with me says the God who is 'altogether beyond mind and being.' Although your understanding is in the way you shall be deified* [made into little gods]; *because your reason is a complete distraction you shall be utterly passive in my presence."* It would be easy to laugh at Dionysius' absurdities but for the fact that his work was popular and influential in providing an important foundation for the mystical (experiential) tradition in both Eastern Orthodoxy and Roman Catholicism. Its bias against the use of the mind in spiritual matters was something which gained credence in some of the more contemplative Monastic Orders. Today, one of the hardest things that the Church will have to do is to come to terms with the unpleasant reality that much of its mystical tradition has rested upon the wrong foundations. Serious errors have occurred in the experiential as well as the doctrinal areas. Certainly, to decry the mind in the way Dionysius did is to preach *'a doctrine of devils.'* This is because any neutralisation of the mind opens it up to satanic

---

[37] This extract was taken from pp. 59-60 of *'The Lion Book of Christian Thought.'* This book is a very useful introduction to both the good and bad currents of thought having existed throughout Church history.

influence. Even now, the trouble with many mystics is that they mistake *'the Angel of light'* for *'divine light'* and *'demonisation'* for *'deification.'* Worst of all, they confuse a *'God'* of their own imagination with the one true God who reveals Himself in scripture. Dionysius' work has left a very harmful legacy by repeating the age-old lie, *"you shall be as gods,"* (Genesis 3:53). No wonder the Lord punished Syrian Christianity by giving it over to Islam. It's easy to imagine that Islam would come as a relief to the sort of nonsense originally taught by Dionysius.

However, perhaps the most striking point to emerge from **Revelation 4:8** is the way in which heavenly worship lends equal weight to the various divine attributes, with no trace at all of *'attribute misfocus.'* *'The Denial Method'* has already implied that viewing the divine attributes in equal proportion can bring about a mature stability to the Christian life. To clarify this point still further it will be necessary in the next chapter to employ: -

1) The Affirmative Method which asks;
"What are the likely logical and practical consequences of affirming the unity between divine holiness and divine love?"

2) The Interactive Method which asks;
"How do the attributes of divine holiness and divine love interact with one another?"

Both methods further demonstrate the unity existing between each of those attributes.

From this section, it's possible to conclude that: -

1) The highest-ranking angels in heaven praise God for being:
1.1 Holy
1.2 Sovereign
1.3 Perfect
1.4 Eternal
1.5 Glorious
1.6 Omnipresent

2) The presence of such enthusiastic worship implies that God is a God of holy-love

3) A direct personal encounter (or series of encounters) with God is characterised by: -

3.1 Sound doctrinal content, which accords with the teaching of scripture

3.2 Feelings of personal unworthiness and helplessness caused by a sense of inner sinfulness

3.3 Joy at the marvellous way in which God reaches out to rescue sinners

3.4 A clear commission to undertake a task or series of tasks that would be normally (or nearly) impossible to accomplish on natural human strength alone[38]

3.5 Greater self-control and clarity of mind

3.6 A heightening of normal human faculties, *i.e.* affecting the will and the intellect

3.7 Respect for human dignity

3.8 Complete control of physical faculties (with a total <u>absence</u> of uncontrolled physical or bodily manifestations, *i.e.* mocking laughter or passive *'zombie-like'* states).

3.9 A reduction of natural self-centredness

Questions

1) What three elements should characterise a true experience of God?

2) On the basis of the evidence provided, outline reasons given for the *'Toronto Blessing.'*

3) Why do you think an experience like the *'Toronto Blessing* should be avoided rather than commended?

---

[38] This is not to deny that God can call His people to do mundane, ordinary things too.

C3:

ANALYSIS AND APPLICATION

42

S1: A Dynamic Relationship

The use of Midrash has confirmed that a dynamic relationship exists between the attributes of divine holiness and divine love. The God who is so holy that even the seraphim have to hide their eyes in His presence is also the God who is compassionate, reaching out to people and cleansing them from their sins. Through holiness God says, *'No you cannot reach me,'* but through love He says, *'Yes, I can reach you.'* If divine holiness makes it impossible for people to reach God, divine love makes it possible for God to reach people. The cruel thing about false religion is that it condemns people to pursue the impossible task of trying to reach God on their own strength. This point also applies to aberrant forms of Christianity where a false *'salvation by works'* gospel is preached. It needs to be more widely realised in the Church that no person on earth can ever reach God. We are all dependent upon divine mercy.

A beginning can be made in understanding this positive relationship between divine holiness and divine love by listing those features common to both. They each: -
1) Arise from the heart of God
2) Constitute an integral part of God's character wherein they influence: -
2.1 The relationships between the Father, Son and Holy Spirit
2.2 God's attitude to creation
2.3 God's plans for saving people from sin
3) Are demonstrated in: -
3.1 The scriptures
3.2 The life, work and death of Jesus
3.3 The lives of those who faithfully follow Jesus
4) Work together in: -
4.1 Separating good from evil
4.2 Uniting all that is good in *'a New Creation'*
4.3 Inspire worship from both angelic and human beings
5) Display a strong degree of *'attribute linkage'*

Both attributes have the same source in God's essential nature and never work in opposition to one another. Even by themselves, the above listed common characteristics should be enough to discredit the view that God's holiness is in opposition to His love. However, for greater clarity, *'The Interactive Method,'* will now be applied in order to show the linkage existing between these two attributes: -

Divine holiness upholds divine love by: -
1) Purifying it so that love does not become confused with lust
2) Setting clear standards of behaviour for divine love to follow, so that it is not mistaken for an amoral benevolence
3) Motivating it, so that love becomes expressed in a powerful and effective manner
4) Balancing it by showing how love is influenced by other attributes, *e.g.* justice and truth
5) Preventing it from being in conflict with other divine attributes, *e.g.* divine wrath

For its part, divine love upholds divine holiness by: -
1) Tempering it with a certain gentleness so that God does not promptly destroy a sinful Creation
2) Acting as the means whereby people are redeemed whilst simultaneously satisfying the demands of divine holiness
3) Channelling it so that it is not expressed in an indiscriminately destructive way to people
4) Balancing it by showing how holiness is influenced by other attributes, *e.g.* goodness and grace
5) Preventing it from manifesting an unfair harshness

The above ten examples of attribute linkage bring together holiness and love into an essential unity, which itself elicits a further number of important points. The first is that <u>divine holiness and divine love are mutually motivating.</u> Deep within the unfathomable depths of God these attributes stir one another into action. A situation exists wherein holiness prompts the expression of love and love the expression of holiness. Together they inspired the work of Jesus, together they met at the cross and together they are able to find expression in the lives of individual believers.

Secondly, their essential unity prevents the *'deification'* of love, (where love is seen as being greater than God). Such deification leads to the view expressed by a certain Methodist minister who claimed (during sermons preached 1989-90) that, *"Love is God."* Hardly surprisingly, he took the unbiblical stance that all religions can reach out to this power of love. He failed to see holiness and love acting as two intimate partners. It should be stressed that both attributes flow from God; they are not <u>above</u> God; and are <u>never</u> greater than God.

Thirdly, the *'The Essentialist Model'* emphasises the harmony existing between each of these divine attributes. Far from being at war with one another, these character traits of God are in a state of complete harmony and equilibrium. Jesus amply demonstrated this essential harmonious unity throughout all of His earthly life. Nowhere was this truer than at Calvary where, by a supreme demonstration of perfect love, Jesus satisfied all of the requirements of God's holiness. *'The Essentialist Model'* is needed to gain a proper understanding of the wonderful work Christ performed at Calvary. Without it the Church is left with a vague, maudlin sentimentality, which never gets to the heart of Man's problem of sin. To lose sight of the underlying unity between divine holiness and love is to lose sight of the Gospel.

Finally, the main value of *'The Interactive Method'* is in its demonstration of how the *'The Essentialist Model'* is vital to Western Christianity – furnishing it with a balanced view of God. Without this view Western Christianity would risk being swamped by all of the evils present within contemporary society. Evidence for this can already be seen in the whole area of sexuality, with growing legal and political pressures to accept homosexual lifestyles in the Church.[39] On an individual level, *'The Essentialist Model'* provides a useful key to spiritual maturity. On a corporate level, a firm grasp of these attributes should enable Churches to offer a more balanced representation of truth. By holding firmly to both divine holiness and divine love, it is possible to grow and develop as a Christian.

This section made it clear that divine holiness and love are united by:

1) Their common characteristics

2) Their ability to uphold one another

3) God's unlimited, almighty power holding both attributes together with no conflict between them

4) Their ability to produce positive results in the lives of individual believers and congregations

---

[39] These are extensively documented by *'The Christian Institute'* at http://www.christian.org.uk

Questions

1) What dangers are likely to arise when people believe that *'love is God?'*

2) List some of the benefits of *'The Essentialist model.'*

3) Describe how a balanced view of divine holiness and divine love promotes spiritual maturity

S2: The Blessing of Balance

Following the analysis of the previous section, it's possible to conclude that the divine attributes of *'holiness'* and *'love'* are *'essential'* rather than *'opposed'* to one another. Also, the recovery of a balanced perspective, giving equal weight to both characteristics is of vital importance to the welfare of Christianity. The neglect of divine holiness has done much to undermine Western Christianity, turning it into a laughing stock in the world.[40] This is because Christians are often only as good as the theology to which they adhere. The more recent history of Western Christianity amply confirms that when Churches go awry in their view of God they often go awry in everything within two or three generations.

However, *'The Affirmative Method'* confirms the essential unity between these two attributes by showing that, for the Christian, they can provide: -:
1) Stoic resilience in the face of hardship and persecution
2) A true and firm faith in Christ, obtained in the power of the Holy Spirit.
3) A flexible but firm Bible-based stance on topical issues
4) <u>Definite</u> moral standards
5) A strong willingness to engage in necessary confrontations whilst avoiding disputes on minor issues
6) A keen interest in the doctrinal teachings and moral instructions of scripture
7) Effective preaching with well-expressed doctrinal content
8) Loving discipline within the Church

---

[40] A non-Christian close relative of mine actually compared the Toronto Experience to a *'boozy'* office party held at the local pub on a late Friday afternoon. This reinforced his unbelief.

9) Wisdom in knowing how to balance tradition with contemporary developments
10) Worship which is both reverent and lively
11) A unity based upon truth rather than expedience or emotionalism
12) Sound organisational and administrative structures
13) An enthusiastic outlook which does not veer wildly into fanaticism

Obviously, other factors, including a willingness to obey God, must also be present in order to guarantee spiritual health. However, employing *'The Affirmative Method'* has suggested that adopting *'The Essentialist Model'* is a first stage towards obtaining this healthy position. A balanced view of divine holiness and love can produce many blessings, not least of which is seeing God as He really is. When this happens, a person is standing in truth rather than in error.

Midrash Bible interpretation enables Christians to see <u>why</u> they are called upon to follow a God of holy-love. His holy-love is the perfect expression of the unity existing between divine holiness and divine love. It shows that the Almighty is fiercely protective of the teachings laid down in scripture, precisely because those teachings reflect His very nature. However, whilst this holy-love gives a resounding *'no'* to human attempts to reach God, it moves the Almighty to such pity for the ruined condition of His Creation that He became a human being in order to reach out to other human beings. Jesus represents God's resounding *'yes!'* to the rescue of sinful humanity. Through everything He did, He challenged all of us to entertain worthy ideas of God. His death also showed that the two attributes of holiness and love, although distinctive, are utterly inseparable. At Calvary, *"the darkness over all the land"* in Matthew 27:45 represented God's unapproachable holiness and His rejection of a mocking, proud religiosity, (Matthew 27:39-41). It also led to a separation between Jesus and His Heavenly Father, as expressed in Christ's agonised cry, *"My God, my God, why have you forsaken me?"* (Matthew 27:46c) However, divine love was demonstrated by the rending of the Temple curtain from top to bottom, showing that God was breaching the barrier between Himself and His creation, (Matthew 27:51). Moreover, this self-giving love was amply demonstrated by Christ's intercession for those who were crucifying Him. With incredible mercy He actually prayed, *"Father, forgive them, for they know not what they do,"* (Luke 23:34a). Love was also revealed by the concern He showed for the dying thief (Luke 23:43) and for His own mother, (John 19:26). By His death, Christ reconciled an unholy, unloving people with the God of holy-love. His success in accomplishing this work demonstrated in a very practical manner the essential unity existing between these two attributes of holiness and love. If Christians grasp this point they are likely to enjoy a fuller picture of who God is. Their reverence for Him will increase and as a result, they will be less inclined to entertain any form of idol in their heart. Exactly what such idols consist of will be explored in the next section.

From this section it's possible to conclude that: -

1) The divine attributes of *'holiness'* and *'love'* are *'essential'* rather than *'opposed'* to one another

2) The recovery of a balanced perspective, apportioning equal weight to both characteristics, is of vital importance to the future welfare of Christianity

3) God's holy-love was amply demonstrated through the events accompanying Christ's death upon the Cross

4) By high lighting His greatness, a comprehensive view of God can help Christians avoid the sin of idolatry

Questions

1) How true is this statement; 'When people or Churches go awry in their view of God they often go awry in everything?' Give reasons for your answer.

2) What factors are needed in order to guarantee the spiritual health of an individual Christian or a congregation?

3) How was God's holy-love demonstrated during the death of Jesus?

S3: Idols in the Heart; What They Are and What to Do About Them

Idolatry can be defined as a harbouring (and a putting into practice) of worthless views about God. Important facets of God's character are ignored, whilst others are overemphasised to an unhelpful degree. It also involves placing one's trust in something or someone other than God. An idol is often no more than a caricature of the real God – with all of the important pieces missing. During the medieval period, the idol was like the real God minus His love, whereas today it resembles the real God minus His holiness. Indeed, an idol is never more dangerous than when it bears a striking resemblance to the one true God. Blatantly false idols like those of Ancient Greece and Rome, eventually became discredited because they were so obviously worthless. In contrast an idol, bearing some resemblance to the real God can enjoy a popularity spanning a whole millennium. This partly explains why Baal was the most dangerous idol facing ancient Israel. Like the true God, Baal made some pretence to claim divine sovereignty, as *'Lord and Master,'* when in reality he represented only the usurping sovereignty of Satan.

Briefly, idols fall into two distinct categories. Firstly, there are the earthly (or worldly) Idols, where an earthly object or person is exalted to some pseudo-divine status. Examples could include the various animal gods of Ancient Egypt or Elvis Presley in the modern world. Indeed, there has recently been a television programme expressly designed for the manufacture of *'Pop Idols.'* Secondly, there are the religious (or spiritual) idols, which resemble the real God minus some important attributes. Within the Church these include the false god of Liberal Theology, (with barely any capacity to communicate God's word to people) and the false god of Mysticism (with little ability to challenge people for their sinfulness).[41] Factions within the wider Church may hold to both types of idols simultaneously, *e.g.* the *'Faith Movement'* where both earthly and religious idols hold sway *i.e.* the *'pop idolatry'* or almost *'hero worship'* of the loudmouthed evangelist, who noisily boasts of his titillating *'spiritual'* experiences.[42] (Alternatively, he may adopt a superficially wholesome *'boy next*

---

[41] Usually, mysticism is far happier to impart *'nice'* experiences to anyone gullible enough to want them.
[42] Specific examples were documented in Hank Hanegraaff's book *'Christianity in Crisis,'* first published in 1993. See his preface to Part One *'Once Upon A Time.'* However, Hanegraaff's ministry has since been subject to some very serious allegations that have resulted in bitter court cases in the USA.

door image' by peddling false teaching in an attractively winsome manner.)[43] Those in the *'Faith Movement'* may sometimes display plenty of *'faith'* but the problem is that their faith is in the wrong God! Also, they appear to have great difficulty in distinguishing true faith from an arrogant, often emotionally charged presumption.

Such factors explain why the most deadly long-term threat to Christianity will come from <u>inside</u> rather than <u>outside</u> the Church. It seems wholly reasonable to suppose that it will be the Church itself, which will offer a version of God so like the real one that it could *'deceive the elect if such a thing were possible,'* (Matthew 24:24b). This is not true of other religious groupings holding to very different views of God. The human race may be approaching a time when a hugely subtle, beguiling *'spirit'* will be unleashed through the Church and into the world. Tragically, the Church will be the spawning ground of a deception eventually wreaking more havoc than either Communism or Nazism. Its ultimate result will be destruction on a global scale, with piles of charred corpses. In the more immediate future, this deception will deceive those who will have no love for the truth, (2 Thessalonians 2:10-12). This incredibly powerful and deceitful false spirit will attempt to draw together the majority of the world's population to worship a god who so closely resembles the true God, <u>that for a time he may deceive some of the elect, despite the fact that he is *not* the true God at all.</u>

The Christian believer really must have the Holy Spirit dwelling within and also possess a working knowledge of scripture in order to withstand the great delusion this other spirit will bring. Again, it must be stressed that this delusion will not be an obvious one (unlike the Toronto Experience, which even the world could see through) but will be far more subtle in nature.[44] Furthermore, it will be nearly-impossible to resist this spirit, should the Christian's heart be divided between following Christ <u>and</u> some form of personal idol – whether it be money, sex and power or even a totem pole in a remote forest clearing. One common result of clinging to a personal idol is the kind of ridiculous behaviour more often associated with those suffering some form of substance addiction. This is because idolatry <u>is</u> a form

---

[43] The motivational evangelist Joel Osteen could well be an example of this; he perhaps represents an attempt by the *'Word of Faith Movement'* to gain respectability amongst the American Evangelical Middle Classes by toning down its presentation. His ministry has been subject to much well documented criticism.

[44] Those who succumbed to the Toronto Deception will stand no chance whatsoever against this far more powerful, deceptive spirit.

of addiction that obsesses and possesses people. Through this sin, Satan tries to grieve God by degrading His Creation (as in the case of human sacrifice). To cling onto idols dismantles inner defences against deception. It can be compared to a spiritual form of *'AIDS'* wherein a person is robbed of immunity to full-scale spiritual harm. Unless believers allow Christ to smash these idols, which so readily spring up within the human heart, they are heading straight for spiritual delusion.

Some of the above points were made in a sermon the writer gave to a *'Young Persons Group'* at an Afro-Caribbean Church on the evening of Tuesday, 14th July 1992.[45] Records kept concerning this meeting show there were 23 (mainly young) people present. At the time, many in the group were being enticed to follow a certain *'white'* false prophet from California.[46] The hope is that readers will be challenged by the following message taken from these same sermon notes. (Its lively manner should help balance the more formal style having hitherto pervaded this work. Incidentally, the terms *'personal idol'* and *'idol in the heart'* are used interchangeably.)

After reading from Genesis 35:1-5, Exodus 20:3, 1 John 5:2 and Revelation 22:14-15 (from the King James Version of the Bible) the main sermon began as follows: -

"An idol is anything which is valued more than the Lord Jesus Christ. Seizing first place in one's loyalties, an idol can either be a person, object, organisation and even a philosophical concept. By nature, idols fill a place in the human heart, which should only be occupied by Jesus. As such they represent a substitute for God.

There are a whole variety of idols, the most common being: -
1) Worldly Idols of pleasure, *such a 'wine, women and song.' These usually derive from the behaviour of fallen human nature.*
2) Demonic Idols of false religion and the occult. *These are often drawn from evil spiritual sources.*
3) Respectable, 'churchy' idols, *which are widely accepted inside Bible believing Christian circles. Deriving from the pride and carnality of believers in Jesus, such idols can include: -*

---

[45] The writer timed it as lasting from 9.05 – 9.40pm.
[46] I gave him the nickname *'Venom Deeplash'* which aptly summed up the devastating nature of his ministry, which was still continuing in 2010.

3.1 *Famous preachers (attracting 'groupies' and acting like 'pop stars')*
3.2 *Material possessions*
3.3 *One's own particular gifting, ministry and organizational affiliation*
3.4 *Personal security*
3.5 *Tradition – always doing things in a certain way*

Clearly, idolatry is a very subtle problem, occurring amongst Christians when they overvalue something in the place of Christ. Their whole perspective has gone awry. In his mercy, God will patiently tolerate a lot of stupidity and even some types of sin amongst His people, but <u>He will never, under any circumstances, tolerate an idol.</u> This is because He wishes to occupy first place in our hearts.

Beyond the effects of inborn sin, exactly why a person chooses to tenaciously cling to an idol may be the result many things, including:
1) *Personal background and experience*
2) *Temperamental disposition*
3) *Ignorance*
4) *A particular church or religious setting where: -*
4.1 *Large groups attract those keen for more personal security*
4.2 *Small groups attract those inordinately proud of their own 'personal ministry' (whatever that might be)*
5) *The enticements of the world, (through the mass media, particularly advertising)*
6) *Satan, who tempts a person to idolatry through: -*
6.1 <u>*False*</u> *teaching,* <u>*false*</u> *religious experiences and* <u>*false*</u> *ideological systems like Nazism and Communism*
6.2 *Compromise with non-Christian belief systems, possibly through some form of inter-faith worship*
6.3 *A whole array of personal temptations*
All this is done with a view to getting people to give most of their time and attention to <u>a</u>nything <u>b</u>ut <u>C</u>hrist. (Note the devil's 'ABC' which is present here.) The gospel itself is denied.

As with their types and causes, the <u>effects</u> of idolatry for the Christian can also vary widely, the most common being: -
1) *Ineffectuality; preoccupied with their idol, Christians may become too paralysed to do anything useful for God. As a result, they lazily sit around doing nothing. A slapdash approach is adopted toward life.*

2) *Misplaced zeal;* having a fanatical enthusiasm for the idol in question.
3) *A narrow and intransigent attitude* – with a harsh stance toward anyone questioning a particular set viewpoint. Idolatrous people can be horribly vicious if they believe their idol is under some form of verbal attack.
4) *'Works of the flesh[47]* (particularly divisiveness) predominating. This means that a Christian work becomes:* -
4.1 *Bogged down in endless problems*
4.2 *Clouded by a 'heavy' atmosphere*
4.3 *Dominated by petty rivalries*
4.4 *Useless; the work either disintegrates altogether or becomes yet another embarrassment littering the Christian scene.*
5) *A mixture of self and spiritual deception, resulting in the following two extremes:* -
5.1 *Laxity – leading to disorderly behaviour.*
5.2 *Legalism – producing an arrogant self-righteousness*
(Incidentally, please note that many heresies or false teachings stem from a persistent determination to cling onto some form of personal idol, with the result that a person is not only wrong, but militantly and dogmatically wrong.)
6) *Love of status, which produces:* -
6.1 *A proud 'don't contradict me' kind of authoritarianism*
6.2 *Affected mannerisms, becoming more 'parsonical than a Parson'*
6.3 *Belligerent discourtesy toward outsiders*
6.4 *'Cover-ups,' allowing problems and sins to fester unresolved for years*
6.5 *'Double standards' with one rule for the leadership and another, (often far harsher rule) for the congregation*
6.6 *Dogmatic adherence to the non-essentials of the Christian faith, (e.g. a certain Pentecostal minister who was very preoccupied with the colour of the robes worn by his choir. Well, I suppose it takes all sorts!)*
6.7 *Total insensitivity to the needs of others*
7) *Reliance upon a 'religious system' with an 'it's always been done this way' mentality, often leading to:* -
7.1 *Cold, formal relationships where hierarchical status is deemed very important*
7.2 *An inability to change or relate appropriately to others*
7.3 *Large bureaucratic institutions with a stifling of personal initiative*

---

[47] These are works that arise out of our old, fallen human nature. As such they don't have the blessing of God.

7.4 *Personal frustration and aggravation (having been unable to express what has really and honestly been felt, for so long)*

However, the Bible accepts that good organisation and administration is important. It is the <u>idolization</u> of a particular mode of organisation which is at fault. Pentecostals fall into this trap just as much as members of the more historical churches. Eventually, idols in the heart destroy people; this is because they prevent them from entering God's Kingdom. Moreover, idols tend to get such a grip over a person's life that nothing else can be seen. Far from controlling the idol in question, the person becomes controlled by it. For the non-Christian there is only ever one remedy for an idol in the heart – to <u>respond to the Gospel of Jesus Christ in repentance and faith.</u> This means trusting Him to give the power to deal with any idols.

8) *For the Christian the following remedies are applicable: -*

8.1 *A willingness to ask difficult questions of themselves; e.g. 'What is the idol in my life?' or 'What could easily become an idol if I allowed it to be?' Indeed, let me now pause and ask you 'What is the idol in <u>your</u> life?' Furthermore, 'Are you willing to allow the Lord to remove it?'*

8.2 *Looking at where this idol is leading in the long-term. By doggedly clinging onto this idol the believer may risk missing out on God's blessing.*

8.3 *Realising a stark choice needs to be made, either Jesus first and the idol second (if it's not harmful in itself – otherwise get rid of it)[48] or the idol first and Jesus absent – no other options exist.*

8.4 *Renunciation, which makes a definite break with the idols in question – allowing for no compromise.*

8.5 *Sharing with other believers who are able to keep things in perspective. If the believer is isolated from fellowship, they are to get 'unisolated' as soon as possible.[49] Fellowship is a must in helping to ensure a healthy Christian lifestyle.*

8.6 *'Feeding on the Word' and sound Christian teaching through Bible Study, which helps develop a clear order of priorities in ones daily life.*

8.7 *Nurturing a healthy spiritual life of prayer and worship with a view to keeping a close walk with the Lord.*

---

[48] This applies to idols like personal talents, friends or family, which are not innately evil – but have been given too great a priority. However, innately harmful idols *i.e.* some form of heretical teaching needs to be ruthlessly dumped.

[49] Sadly, the gradual decline in the UK Churches, having continued unabated since this message was given, means that this advice may prove quite difficult to follow. An increasing number of believers are finding themselves in an isolated position through no fault of their own.

8.8 *Developing one's personal gifts and ministries – simply becoming too busy in the Lord to dally with idols.*
8.9 *Taking 'time out' from Christian service in order to regain a sense of perspective.*
8.10 *Looking toward the needs of others, both inside and outside of one's own grouping. This should prevent any morbid introspection, which can lead to idolatry.*
If anyone desires to be used by God to spread the Gospel, then they must put away all idols. Most certainly, a decisive, no nonsense approach is needed. Please do not be one of those people who fool around with idols. As it says in Exodus 20:3 'You shall have no other Gods but me.'

In the name of Jesus Christ our Saviour, Amen"

As the writer finished speaking, the look on people's faces indicated that a deep conviction was present. Nevertheless, over time most of the warnings were to go unheeded, resulting in division within the assembly and immorality amongst former members. Evidence of spiritual delusion was also present in that participants thought that a major revival was about to happen, but it didn't. This group was to demonstrate that the idols followed by many nominal Christians are there to make their devotees *'feel good'* through the provision of free entertainment and the impartation of *'nice feelings.'* Particularly in Pentecostal groups, this idol can barely be distinguished from Bacchus, the Roman God of wine and revelry, the only difference being that the drunkenness is of a spiritual rather than an alcoholic nature.

From this section it is possible to conclude that: -

1) A personal idol is any loyalty which replaces God in one's innermost being

2) The main types of idols are: -
2.1 Worldly idols
2.2 Demonic idols
2.3 *'Churchy'* idols

3) The causes of idolatry are: -
3.1 Individual personal weaknesses
3.2 Ignorance of the truth
3.3 Organisational pressures

3.4 The influence of the world or fallen human society
3.5 Satan, working through a variety of temptations and spiritual seductions

4) Some common effects of personal idols are: -
4.1 Ineffectuality in Christian service
4.2 Misplaced zeal
4.3 The *'works of the flesh'*[50] predominating
4.4 Heightened vulnerability to spiritual deception
4.5 An unhealthy dependence upon a religious system
4.6 Eternal destruction

5) For non-believers the only cure for idolatry is a fully committed faith in Jesus Christ as Lord and Saviour

6) Every believer has a responsibility to co-operate with Jesus in the removal of personal idols by: -
6.1 Allowing Jesus to remove any personal idol as soon as it is exposed
6.2 Giving serious thought to the likely long-term consequences of following an idol
6.3 Accepting that a choice exists between Jesus and the personal idol in question
6.4 Making a definite decision to renounce an idol
6.5 Sharing fellowship with other believers
6.6 Feeding on sound Bible-based teaching
6.7 Nurturing a healthy spiritual life of prayer and worship
6.8 Keeping busy, constructively and/or creatively
6.9 Taking *'time out'* to rest and to gain a sense of perspective
6.10 Looking to meet the needs of others

Questions

1) What is an idol?

2) What are the causes and effects of idolatry?

3) Why might believers be unwilling to allow Jesus to remove an idol from their heart?

4) How can we abandon personal idols? What blessings may result from doing this?

---

[50] *I.e.* those that originate in unregenerate human nature

CONCLUSION

For those preferring not to view God as a God of inseparable holiness and love, there can appear to exist a tangible conflict within the Godhead. They would rather choose to assent to this less than perfect God than acknowledge the fundamental unity which binds these two attributes flawlessly together. These very same people (mainly in the Western Church) are now paying dearly for holding such an erroneous view. It has led them to serving, not the God of scripture, but a fabricated caricature, one derived from their own imagination. For them, divine holiness has been largely ousted in favour of divine love which itself seems little more than a trite form of sentimentality. God is viewed as something of an over-indulgent *'sugar daddy'* that can be easily coerced into giving His children anything they ask for. The very words *'God is love'* (1 John 4:8b) have been plucked out of scripture and turned inside out to read *'love is God.'*[51] Within many churches this has become the widely accepted yet completely fabricated and grotesque caricature. Especially in the Western World, this subtle twist of words, left unchallenged for so long, has led to a bland and powerless form of Christianity. Love has taken centre stage with most of the other divine attributes unceremoniously pushed out to the wings. One problem with such a caricature is that it cannot save people from their sins nor give them eternal life. Quite the reverse is true; by distracting attention away from the real God it has procured damnation for many. A role reversal has taken place where the concept of love has superseded God Himself. *'Love is God'* has taken the pre-eminence with all of God's other divine attributes largely negated. The very idea that an utterly holy God could even think of acting in wrathful judgement is simply an anathema – after all, surely His great *'love'* would prevent Him from behaving in such a condemnatory way? From this standpoint, the whole concept of a wrathful God just wouldn't make sense. The soft, pliable *'sugar daddy'* suddenly deciding to chastise his children for some misdemeanour is viewed as being completely impossible. That God would allow any hurt to His children is just something which cannot be contemplated. This incorrect *'love is God'* view has gone deep

---

[51] The writer vividly recalls one particular Methodist Minister who (in the late 1980's) would repeatedly use this phrase. His theology was very liberal and his tedious sermons had no other theme than that of God as loving creator. He and his wife were extremely resistant to the gospel. The meditation *'Whole Counsel'* which forms the prologue of *'The Leeds Liturgy'* was written with them very much in mind.

into the human psyche – to admit that He can, in His Holiness, fulfil the role of wrathful judge demands a return to biblical thinking. Repentance and faith in the God of scripture are the only means whereby gaps in knowledge and incorrect views can be evaluated and put right.

Seriously incorrect views of God leave both individuals and Churches mentally unprepared to face any outworking of divine wrath, should it ever happen. At such a time God's holiness (for so long ignored) will suddenly be brought sharply into relief. God's wrath will be played out in its own way and its own time, and when it does happen many inside the Church will receive a *'blasting'* rather than a *'blessing.'* This will result in a disowning and even a denying of Christ altogether.[52] A clear understanding of God's holiness may well be reached by some – but often at the cost of much unnecessary heartbreak and distress. Love has been over-emphasised for so long that when wrath and subsequent judgement really do appear the reaction will often be one of shock, anger and denial. Many will even dare to wag their finger at God, wondering how such a loving God could act in this way. Others will react in abject sadness and total confusion. Either way there will have been a complete failure to accept that wrath can be an expression of outraged love or when faced with evil, wrath may prove to be the most appropriate response – not least because it motivates God to forcibly remove the evil in question. Thankfully, amidst God's wrath a few Christians will be forced to totally re-appraise their view of the deity. They will come to realize that what they'd previously thought concerning God's character simply wasn't sufficiently biblical to cover such a development. Their previously held notion of the apparent internal conflict between God's attributes will come to be realized for what it is – a *'phantom conflict'* – real only in the minds of those wanting it to be there. It's to be hoped that a drastic change in mind and heart (repentance) will be the positive outcome of such a profound appraisal. It really does need to become clear to each and every Christian that the divine attributes of holiness and love are inextricably bound together, the one harmoniously interwoven with the other. When viewed in this correct and wholly scriptural way God's wrath and judgement will begin to make sense. What once was viewed as a severe internal conflict between divine holiness and

---

[52] This may follow a period of shock and outright disbelief that their *'God of love'* could even be remotely displeased with them. How could He act in such a wrathful way? What has a God of love to do with wrath anyway?

divine love will be a conflict no more. It will disappear like a lifting morning mist. Divine wrath will be seen for what it really is – an appropriate expression of outraged love against human sinfulness and evil. At the individual level, repentance and faith in the gospel message that Christ died to atone (cover) our sins is the surest way to pacify this wrath. Christ's death and resurrection brought <u>all</u> of the divine attributes into focus. It was then that God's wrath against sin was appeased and all of His attributes were clearly displayed in their complete harmony. Any conflict (whether real or imagined) is quelled at the cross of Christ. In this context, it's helpful to note that God is too perfect to be ever at war within Himself. Peacefulness has been a core of attribute of His from all eternity.

Regaining Spiritual Health

If Western Christianity is to regain any degree of spiritual health it must adopt a balanced, scriptural view of divine holiness and love. This ought to be a priority because exactly how we view God influences our daily living which also affects the quality of our Church life. After all, a single Christian is always part of the *'body of Christ,'* which in this context means the Church. Should a Christian's views about God be wrong or imbalanced the result is a defective Christianity which at best is powerless and at worst is downright malignant. Holding to a correct Biblically-based view of God involves far more than just accepting an abstract theory or doctrine; it's something which can radically affect each and every single Christian. Admittedly, the recovering of a balanced view of divine holiness and divine love is <u>not</u> sufficient in itself for a complete re-gaining of spiritual health, but it certainly represents a necessary beginning.

Having focused upon the harmonious unity of divine holiness and love, a detailed summary of biblical teaching concerning this subject can be found in **Appendix 1.** This is followed by bible-based confessional *'summaries of faith'* which vividly describe this very close relationship – see **Appendices 2-3.** A more abstract summary of this relationship will be found in **Appendix 4.** Different ways to test whether such a unity really does exist are listed in **Appendix 5.**

Facing God

On Judgement Day, every human being will have to face God, either in His inapproachable holiness (as unredeemed sinners) or in His approachable love (as saints whose sins have been forgiven). On that Day they will discover whether they are either *'vessels of wrath'* or *'vessels of mercy,'* (Romans 9:22-23). There is no in-between state. To be a *'vessel of mercy'* will have required the definite belief that, through His sacrificial death upon the cross, Jesus fully appeased God's (justified) wrath against sin and opened the way to His Father's mercy and grace. Such faith is <u>the only sure means</u> of receiving complete forgiveness and eternal life; there is <u>no</u> other way to know God. To believe otherwise is to be in a state of delusion. Should you, the reader wish to receive this faith then the following *'prayer of commitment'* (taken from **Section 8A** of the writer's other book *'The Leeds Liturgy'*) may prove helpful;

"Lord Jesus Christ, Son of God (Mark 1:1)
Have mercy upon me, a sinner (Matthew 15:22 & 20:30)
And please give me
That relationship with God your Father (John 14:6)
That only you can provide (Acts 4:12)

Please, come into my life
Please, come into my heart and mind (Revelation 3:20)
Please, come in to deal with my every sin
And Father, send your Holy Spirit (Luke 11:13)
To remove any fear, doubt, confusion and unbelief (2 Timothy 1:7)

Relying upon <u>your</u> strength alone (Zechariah 4:6)
I willingly accept you (John 1:12)
As my Saviour, Lord and God (1 Timothy 1:15)
Who died upon the cross (Matthew 27:50)
To take the punishment I deserved for my sin
And who, three days later, rose bodily from the dead (Romans 10:9)

So, thank you Jesus, Son of God (1 John 4:15)
For having mercy upon me
And for giving me a relationship
With God as my Father (2 Corinthians 5:21)
From now on, Lord Jesus (1 Corinthians 12:3)
I willingly commit myself to you
And to obeying your will (Acts 5:29)
For the rest of my life, Amen"

Anyone looking up the term *'The Sinner's Prayer'* (another name for *'The prayer of commitment'*) on the Internet will know that the use of this type of prayer is controversial. This is because it has tended to be viewed as something of a magic ritual with the power (just by being spoken) of conferring salvation. Because of this magical connotation some preachers have even accused it of damning millions to Hell! It's also been criticised on the grounds of it having derived solely from evangelical tradition rather than from scripture alone. Such criticisms rightly point out that the Gospels and Epistles repeatedly stress that <u>salvation from sin is only ever to be found through faith (which is that God-given, humble, dependent trust in Christ) and not through a superstitious reliance upon a particular prayer 'formula,' no matter how bible-based it may be.</u> Without this genuine faith in Christ a person can repeat *'The Sinner's Prayer'* over and over again and still spend a lost eternity in Hell. (This is because it will have become nothing more than a mantra or a self-justifying religious performance.) However, on a more positive note what such a prayer <u>can do</u> is to put into words a faith which has already been planted in the human heart by the Holy Spirit. It marks *'a rite of passage'* from eternal death to eternal life. In this context, if full trust[53] is placed in Jesus' death and resurrection eternal life is received as a wonderful free gift from God. Enormous comfort can be drawn from the promise of Romans 10:9 which guarantees that, *"If you confess with your mouth the Lord Jesus Christ and believe in your heart that God has raised Him from the dead you <u>will</u> be saved."* *'The prayer of commitment'* holds great value in helping those who may find verbal articulation a little daunting when attempting to apply the promise made in this verse. It provides something clear and concise to *'confess with the mouth'* and expresses the belief already existing within that person's heart. When used in this way, such a prayer can be hugely beneficial in practically applying the truths of scripture. It helps a new believer to receive the assurance that they have been rescued from their sins and that eternal life is now theirs.

Through faith we receive (as a gracious free gift) a life-changing relationship with God.[54] We begin to place our complete trust and confidence in God and His Word, (The Bible). At the human level, we know that all healthy inter-personal relationships are built upon this hugely important element of trust. It is the bedrock upon which all else stands, including the world economy. Through faith in Christ, we

---

[53] This means believing with the *'heart'* as well the *'head.'* In other words, it's a faith that must engage every level of our personality.

[54] In passing, it's worth stressing that faith is the quality needed to underpin any constructive personal relationship, whether with God or with other people. Without this quality no friendship or healthy marital and family life could even remotely exist. Each individual would be left isolated by their own mistrust of others.

come to know God in the fullness of His love rather than His wrath. Having repented (turned away from our sin) and turned to Christ we now have a solid and steadfast foundation upon which to build our lives. This is exactly the time when we need to turn to scripture to obtain as accurate and as clear a picture of who God is. After all, when a new friendship is formed it's only right to get to know that person a little more. Our trust in God increases as we learn to rely upon what He says in Scripture. We place our faith (confident trust) in His promises, one of which informs us that *"all things work together for good to them that love God."* (Romans 8:28a). Also, a greater trust is gained as we see God at work in our lives (often amidst very difficult circumstances) and our friendship with Him develops throughout the subsequent years. We find that God really is *'as good as His Word.'*[55]

Practical Helps

Practical *'helps'* on how to grow in the Christian faith will be found in **Section 27** of *'The Leeds Liturgy.'* However, for the new Christian, the following points should prove useful: -
1) Receive water baptism (full immersion)[56] in the name of *'The Father, the Son and the Holy Spirit,'* as commanded by Christ, (Matthew 28:19)
2) Ask God to increase your faith and your understanding of the Bible
3) Inform other responsible Christians about your new-found faith in Christ
4) Use all available media to become better informed about the teachings of Christianity – these are summarised in the Apostles and Nicene Creeds and in the Protestant Confessions of faith like the Westminster Confession (1646) and the Baptist Confession (1689)
5) Develop the daily habit of praying to Him and reading His Word (beginning with the Gospels and Epistles)
6) Seek fellowship with other genuine followers of Jesus
7) Find a sane, Bible-based (preferably local) church where you can worship God and receive good teaching

---

[55] There's also the added point that to become (and to remain) a Christian is to be committed to a life of constant trust and learning – for there's always more to learn about God and His ways. In one sense, every Christian is a perpetual student.
[56] For those who are severely disabled water baptism may best be achieved by pouring water upon the head and body. Sensitive pastoral care will be needed from all involved parties, whether elders or others in the congregation.

8) Network with a group of believing friends who can answer any questions and provide practical and/or pastoral support
9) Invest in a Bible, a simple Bible Concordance and a Bible Dictionary
10) Foster a healthy, enquiring attitude that queries anything supposedly said or done in the name of God or Christ. (Avoid literature promising easy ways to get rich and healthy.)

Perhaps the first step of all is to thank God for such a wonderful salvation. You now know God as your approachable and loving Heavenly Father. He's no longer the wrathful judge, whose inapproachable holiness means that He must forever banish you from His presence. In light of this blessing it seems appropriate to close with the following meditation: -

Thank you God for your great salvation
Thank you God for your great redemption
Thank you God for your great deliverance
Thank you God for being God –
The God of holy-love[57]

Truly, all believers in Christ have much to be thankful for.

Questions

1) How do the attributes of divine holiness and divine love complement one another?

2) What are the likely problems to arise from ignoring the unity of divine holiness and divine love?

3) Why is faith in Jesus so important in getting to know God?

---

[57] Entitled, *'Thanksgiving,'* this meditation was written on Saturday, 6th November 2010.

APPENDICES
CONFESSIONAL AND OTHER SUMMARIES

"Humility is usually an older person's virtue. Young people are often too full of themselves to see the need for it."[58]

---

[58] The author, Thursday, 13 January 2000

A1:

BIBLICAL TEACHING ON DIVINE HOLINESS AND DIVINE LOVE

Shaded rows with bold lettering denote those passages used in the Parashiyot and Peshar Midrash or in the Introductory Comments.

The scriptures teach that divine holiness (or purity): -

1 Keeps God separate and distant from humanity	Ex	3:5
2 Destroys those people who try to approach God by their own efforts		19:21
3 Prevents both people & priests from ascending to God		24
4 Requires that someone in a *'Priestly Office'* make atonement for sin	Lev	17:32
5 Is proclaimed by God		21:8
6 Warns that God's Holy Name is not to be profaned		22:2
7 Motivates the divine jealousy that punishes sin	**Jos**	**24:19**
8 Demonstrates that, *'There is none as holy as the Lord'*	1S	2:2
9 Brings awareness of the gulf existing between a *'holy God'* and humanity		6:20
10 Encourages worshipping Jews to *'Glory in His holy Name'*	1Ch	16:10
11 Incites worshipping Jews to *'give thanks to* [His] *holy Name'*		35
12 Prompts the Lord to save David, *'His anointed King,'* from trouble	Ps	20:6
13 Can be acknowledged during times of great suffering and rejection		22:3
14 Provokes a joyful trust in His Holy Name		33:21
15 Should inspire people to praise God's *'Great and terrible Name'*		**99:3**
16 Can promote an exultant worship, *'for He is Holy'*		5
17 Highlights the fact that *'The Lord our God is holy'*		**9**
18 Enables people to *'Bless His holy Name'*		103:1
19 Realises the hope of redemption from evil		111:9
20 Confirms that *'The Lord is holy in all His works'*		145:17
21 Exhorts *'all flesh* [to] *bless His holy Name forever'*		21
22 Proclaims that *'the knowledge of the holy* [Lord] *is understanding'*	Pr	9:9
23 Exposes human ignorance on spiritual matters		30:3
24 Expresses itself in righteous judgements	Is	5:16
25 Provokes endless angelic worship directed toward God Himself		**6:3**
26 Is displayed by God's almighty power		52:10
27 Can indwell those of *'a contrite and humble spirit'*		57:10
28 Confronts the idolatry of those who rebel against God's Holy name	Ezk	20:39
29 Leads God to oppose those who discredit His name amongst the heathen		36:20
30 Allows God to have pity for His people		21

31 Provokes compassion for a wayward people		22
32 Means that both Jews and Gentiles will know that God is holy		39:7
33 Means that Israel will no longer defile God's Holy Name		43:7
34 Means that to defile God's Holy Name is to provoke divine anger		8
35 Is defiled by both social injustice and sexual immorality	Am	2:7

37 Causes Christians to know when to refrain from being 'holier than thou'	Mt	7:6
38 **Secures the goodness of God**	**Mk**	**10:18**
39 Allowed Mary to declare 'Holy is His Name'	Lu	1:49
40 Causes Jesus to pray to His 'Holy Father' for the safety of His disciples	Joh	17:11
41 Is displayed by the outpouring of God's Holy Spirit	Acts	2:4
42 Is highlighted by the Spirit of holiness	Rom	1:4
43 Is to be reflected in the lives of congregational elders and deacons	Ti	1:8
44 Exhorts people to build themselves up in their 'most holy faith'	Jude	20
45 Is continually celebrated by the highest-ranking angels in heaven	Rev	4:8

For further Bible references, please refer to a Concordance and look up the words, 'Holy Ghost,' 'Holy One' and 'Holy One of Israel' 'Holy Name,' 'Holy Spirit', 'my wrath' and 'wrath of God.'

The scriptures teach that divine love (or compassion): -

1 Motivated God's selection of the Israelites to be His people	De	7:7
2 Bestows many blessings		7:13
3 Will lead to the eventual restoration of Israel into a place of blessing		30:3
4 Inspires prayer	1K	8:50
5 **Turns away divine anger from a disobedient people**	**2K**	**13:23**
6 Inspires God to deliver people from a variety of perils	Ps	91:14
7 Leads to a godly reverence		103:18
8 Causes God to comfort Israel	Is	43:4
9 **Is shown by God's pity for afflicted people**		**63:9**
10 Never fails	La	3:22
11 Is revealed in God's pity for His people Israel	Joel	2:18
12 Is revealed in God's pity for the pagans of Nineveh	Jon	4:11
13 Will subdue our iniquities by working in our hearts	Mic	7:19
14 Prompts God to rejoice over His people with singing	Zep	3:17

15 Was expressed in the care given by Jesus to needy individuals	Mt	9:22
16 Was expressed in the care given by Jesus to a needy multitude		15:32
17 Motivated Jesus to heal the blind and the lame		21:14
18 Motivated Jesus to warn His disciples against deception		24:4
19 Motivated Jesus to cast out demons	Mk	1:34
20 Motivated Jesus to heal the deaf and dumb		7:37
21 Is to be expressed in humble service		10:43
22 Was highlighted by the parable of the prodigal son	Lu	15:20
23 Was shown by God the Father in sending His Son Jesus into the World	Joh	3:16
24 Rebukes religious people who do not have God's love in them		5:42
25 Emphasises the responsibility of all believers to abide in God's love		15:10
26 Can be poured into the hearts of believers	Rom	5:5
27 Was shown in the manner in which Jesus died for sinners		8
28 Allows nothing to separate it from believers		8:34
29 Is selectively revealed to believers		9:15
30 Can inspire the wording of specific prayers	2Co	13:14
31 Directs our hearts into 'the love of God'	2Th	3:5
32 Was manifested through Jesus Christ	Ti	3:4
33 'Can have compassion on the ignorant' who are unaware of the truth	Heb	5:2
34 Can be demonstrated through the love Christians show for one another	1Pet	3:8
35 Is shown by those who 'keep His word'	1Joh	2:5
36 Had its ultimate manifestation in the death of Jesus		3:16
37 Should prompt Christians to show compassion for the poor		17
38 By definition, is one of the attributes of God		4:8
39 Was proven, by God sending His Son 'into the World so that we may live' in Him		:9
40 Gives Christians a responsibility to 'love one another'		4:12
41 Leads believers to keep God's commandments		5:3
42 Exhorts Christians to keep themselves 'in the love of God'	Jude	21
43 Highlights the need for compassion to be shown in disagreements		22
44 Emphasises that Jesus should be the 'first love' of every Church	Rev	2:4

For further Bible references, please refer to a Concordance and look up the words, 'compassion,' 'his love,' 'love of God,' 'loving kindness' and 'mercy.'

A2: QUESTION AND ANSWER SUMMARY

Q1 *"What is divine holiness?"*

A1 *"It is God's absolute moral purity and inapproachable separation from anything flawed, sinful or evil. It makes it impossible for people to reach God."*

Q2 *"What is divine love?"*

A2 *"It is God's absolute compassion and rational, selfless kindness shown toward his Creation."*

Q3 *"What is holy-love?"*

A3 *"It is an absolutely pure compassion. It means that, whilst God will not compromise His perfect moral standards (as revealed in scripture) He will show pity to those who turn from their sins and put their trust in His Son, Jesus Christ."*

Q4 *"How does divine holiness and divine love differ?"*

A4 *"Divine holiness emphasises God's moral purity and inapproachability; whilst divine love emphasises His tenderness and willingness to reach out to His Creation."*

Q5 *"Do such differences mean that these attributes are in conflict with one another?"*

A5 *"No, they only appear to be in conflict (a 'phantom' conflict) because sinful human beings find it difficult to grasp how God could possibly maintain such diverse characteristics and yet remain thoroughly united in His innermost Being. Furthermore, sinful humanity would perhaps rather view God as flawed in some way preferring instead to emphasise this apparent conflict. After all if God isn't perfect, then He can't blame sinful humanity for its imperfections either!"*

Q6 *"What dangers are likely to arise in a situation where divine holiness and divine love are persistently viewed as being in conflict with one another?"*

A6 *"Should these attributes be viewed in conflict then God suddenly becomes imperfect and can no longer be regarded as God – for, by definition, God is perfect (completely free from any fault and utterly flawless in every aspect of His nature)."*

Q7 *"What are the likely long-term consequences should divine holiness alone be overlooked?"*

A7 *"Should divine holiness be overlooked then the likely long-term consequences include a 'religion of frivolity' where God's presence is entered into in a casual, almost convivial manner. There is no sense of inner sinfulness and therefore no need for repentance."*

Q8 *"What are the likely long term consequences should divine love alone be overlooked?"*

A8 *"Should divine love be overlooked then the likely long-term consequences include a 'religion of fear' wherein substitute mediators (like the Virgin Mary or the Saints) are actively sought to appease an angry and remote God."*

Q9 *"What are the likely long-term consequences should the existence of both divine holiness and love be overlooked?"*

A9 *"The likely long-term consequences if both divine attributes are overlooked include a religion where God is viewed as an impersonal cosmic force (like electricity), resulting in people leading their lives as if He didn't exist at all. (A cosmic force is not a person, thereby precluding any chance of a personal relationship, let alone repentance.)"*

Q10 *"How do we definitely know that divine holiness and love are united to one another?"*

A10 *"Divine holiness and divine love are united to one another because they: -*
- *Are revealed throughout the Old and New Testaments*
- *Are a definite part of God's character*
- *Are bound together by God's almighty unlimited power*
- *Work together to separate good from evil*
- *Work together to unite all that is good*
- *Are jointly able to arouse angelic as well as human worship*
- *Mutually strengthening and motivate one another*

- *Are amply demonstrated in the life and death of Jesus*
- *Produce good results in the lives of individual believers and congregations"*

Q11 *"What are the likely benefits should both attributes be consistently viewed as being united?"*

A11 *"The likely benefits are: -*
- *A true and settled faith in Christ with the Holy Spirit indwelling the believer*
- *Resilience in the face of hardship and persecution*
- *A flexible but firm Bible-based stance on topical issues*
- *Definite positive moral standards*
- *A willingness to engage in necessary confrontations whilst avoiding disputes on minor issues*
- *An active interest in the doctrinal teachings and moral instructions of scripture*
- *Effective preaching with well-expressed doctrinal content*
- *Loving discipline within the Church*
- *Wisdom in knowing how to balance tradition with contemporary developments*
- *A worship that is reverent but lively*
- *A Christian unity based upon truth rather than expedience or emotionalism*
- *Sound organisational and administrative structures*
- *An enthusiastic discipline, which is definitely not fanatical"*

Q12 *"Is it true that the Old Testament majors upon God's holiness whilst the New majors upon His love?"*

A12 *"Although this statement does contain an element of truth, it must be stressed that both Testaments reveal both attributes. However, a greater revelation for love is granted in the New Testament because it is here that God's love in sending his Son to die on behalf of sinful humanity is made transparently explicit. In contrast, divine holiness is consistently emphasised throughout the Old Testament – through the ordinances of the Mosaic Law and in the divine judgements implemented against those who trespassed against that same law."*

Q13 *"What are the characteristics of a true experience of God?"*

A13 *"A true experience of God contains the following characteristics:*
- *A person becomes more humane and self-controlled in behaviour*
- *An enthusiasm for Bible-based teaching*
- *An intransigent attitude toward falsehood*
- *A strengthening of the mind with an enlargement of intellectual faculties*
- *A firm sense of emotional stability*
- *Greater self-control, once the initial surprise of the experience has faded*
- *A positive inner attitude and willingness to grow in the things of God*
- *A desire to reach out to others with the truth*
- *Practical service on behalf of others*
- *A wise and calm use of the 'laying on of hands' during a healing ministry"*

Q14 *"What are the characteristics of a false religious experience?"*

A14 *"A false religious experience often contains the following characteristics: -*
- *It dehumanises people by rendering them passive (and sometimes ridiculous in their behaviour)*
- *Important Biblical teachings are purposefully ignored*
- *False teaching is tolerated and false teachers often slavishly followed*
- *The mind is 'switched off' and anything spiritual in content passively accepted*
- *Extreme and often very sudden mood swings*
- *Diminished self-control, sometimes resulting in acts of sexual immorality*
- *Addiction to pleasurable experiences alone, resulting in a lack of true spiritual growth*
- *A centring upon the 'self" and an inner desire for self-gratification. This may be accompanied by a near obsessive compulsion to 'pass on' the experience and the false teachings associated with it, often through the indiscriminate 'laying on of hands.'"*

Q15 *"Does God expect us to use our minds when undergoing a true religious experience?"*

A15 *"Yes, He does!"*

Q16 *"Why may Christians be unwilling to use their minds during a religious experience?"*

A16 *"Because they may be: -*
- *Blindly following the example of their leaders*
- *Influenced by false teaching*
- *Bound up in various personal problems*
- *Young in the faith*
- *Badly instructed in the things of God*
- *Lazy, fearful or impatient in wanting 'instant gratification'"*

Q17 *"How are such people to be handled?"*

A17 *"They should be correctly taught and warned (either gently or firmly) that the Lord requires them to use their minds when encountering Him. In addition, they may need to examine whether they really are true believers – who have they definitely trusted Christ as their Saviour? In certain cases, care for pastoral problems may also prove helpful."*

Q18 *"Why would the devil wish to encourage people to make little or no use of their minds during a religious experience?"*

A18 *"Because he wants to deceive them, to actively work through them and to spoil their chances of receiving eternal life"*

Q19 *"How should we react to any teaching (or practice) which encourages people not to use their minds?"*

A19 *"We should firmly reject it as being utterly false – no matter how pleasant or useful it may sound."*

Q20 *"Did Jesus die at Calvary to reconcile these two attributes of holiness and love?"*

A20 *"No He died to reconcile people to God. However, through His death He demonstrated the eternally existing, perfect unity between divine holiness and love."*

Q21 *"Is a balanced perspective of both God's holiness and love necessary for the welfare of the Church?"*

A21 *"Yes, most certainly!"*

Q22 *"What may happen if a balanced perspective is absent over a protracted period of time?"*

A22 *"The Church will fall and the Gospel will not be proclaimed in its entirety."*

Q23 *"Will recovering a balanced perspective be sufficient to ensure the spiritual well-being of God's people?"*

A23 *"Not necessarily, as there could be other problems hindering the presentation of the Gospel. However, it would represent a necessary first (and major) step in the recovery of a sound and wholesome Christian witness."*

Q24 *"How could this recovery of a sound Christian witness best be put into practice?"*

A24 *"Through prayer and the teaching of God's Word in the power of the Holy Spirit."*

A3: CONFESSIONAL SUMMARY

1) I (we) firmly believe, (without the slightest trace of doubt or secret reservation) that God is flawlessly perfect in both His nature and work. This absolute perfection means that He is completely free from any internal conflict. He is at peace within Himself.

2) I (we) firmly believe, (without the slightest trace of doubt or secret reservation) in the complex rather than the simple unity of God. This complex unity shows that God can easily: -
2:1 Hold together an infinite number of diverse attributes in one unified whole
2:2 Consist of a Trinity of three Persons in one union

3) I (we) firmly believe, (without the slightest trace of doubt or secret reservation) that God is both absolutely holy and absolutely loving. Furthermore, it is acknowledged that both of these attributes co-exist in perfect harmony (without any degree of conflict between them).

4) I (we) firmly believe, (without the slightest trace of doubt or secret reservation) that, as well as having unlimited power, God is a personal Being who possesses (to an infinite degree) personal qualities such as the ability to think, feel, and make decisions and to relate to others in a deeply personal way.

5) I (we) firmly deny, (willingly repudiate and militantly resist) any view that: -
5:1 Divine holiness and love are in opposition to one another
5:2 Divine holiness is revealed only in the Old Testament and divine love only in the New
5:3 Christ's death was intended to reconcile the fundamentally opposed attributes of divine holiness and divine love
5:4 Any form of conflict can ever exist within God's perfect character

6) I (we) firmly believe, (without the slightest trace of doubt or secret reservation) that God's absolute power is able to: -
6:1 Unify the divine attributes of holiness and love
6:2 Reach out and help people
6:3 Enhance normal human attributes *i.e.* the ability to think, feel, make decisions and socialise with others

7) I (we) firmly deny, (willingly repudiate and militantly resist) any view that encourages the belief that (except possibly as a severe judgement of sin – Isaiah 29:9-12) divine power dehumanises people by causing them to behave in a ridiculous way or by reducing them to a state of stupefied passivity. To suggest that the God of holy-love would do such things in order to bless His people is to commit a perverse blasphemy.

8) I (we) firmly believe, (without the slightest trace of doubt or secret reservation) that whilst people are unable to approach God because of the presence of sinful imperfections in their own lives, God has the power, will and motivation to reach out to sinful people.

9) I (we) firmly believe, (without the slightest trace of doubt or secret reservation) that, in gospel preaching, divine holiness is normally stressed <u>before</u> divine love to awaken people to the dreadful reality of their inborn sinfulness. However, in cases where special medical and pastoral needs are present then divine love may well act as the starting point.

10) I (we) firmly believe, (without the slightest trace of doubt or secret reservation) that both individual believers and the wider Church have a responsibility to preserve a balanced perspective regarding divine holiness and divine love. Should such a balance be lost this inevitably results in a loss of faith in the Jesus revealed in scripture. It is acknowledged that viewing the attributes of divine holiness and love in opposition to one another has been responsible for seriously weakening the life and testimony of the Church.

11) I (we) firmly believe, (without the slightest trace of doubt or secret reservation) that divine holiness upholds divine love by: -
11:1 Purifying it, so that love does not become confused with lust
11:2 Setting objective standards for love to follow, so that it is not mistaken for an amoral benevolence
11:3 Motivating it, so that love becomes expressed in a powerful and effective manner
11:4 Allowing love to be further influenced by other attributes like justice and truth
11:5 Preventing love from being in conflict with other divine attributes like divine wrath (as because of God's love judgement and wrath must come)

12) I (we) firmly believe, (without the slightest trace of doubt or secret reservation) that divine love upholds divine holiness by: -
12:1 Tempering it with gentleness so that God does not promptly destroy a sinful Creation
12:2 Devising a means (Christ's death upon the cross) whereby sinful people are redeemed and rescued from God's wrath and indignation
12:3 Channelling it – ensuring it is not expressed in such a way that it would destroy people
12:4 Causing it to be balanced by other attributes, *e.g.* goodness and grace
12:5 Preventing it from being confused with an unfair harshness

13) I (we) firmly believe, (without the slightest trace of doubt or secret reservation) that divine holiness is often expressed through the wrathful judgements of God. In contrast, divine love is often expressed through the gracious mercy of God, *e.g.* His holding in place an imperfect universe and allowing even unregenerate people to enjoy a measure of blessing.

14) I (we) firmly believe, (without the slightest trace of doubt or secret reservation) that, by His death, Jesus fully satisfied the requirements of divine holiness. At the same time, He opened up a way whereby people could receive all of the blessings of divine love. He fully demonstrated the essential unity existing between these two attributes.

15) I (we) firmly believe, (without the slightest trace of doubt or secret reservation) that, in God, the attributes of holiness and love are mutually motivating. Hence, where one of these characteristics is manifested so also is the other. Indeed they are so inseparable that it is fitting to use the term *'holy-love.'*

16) I (we) firmly believe, (without the slightest trace of doubt or secret reservation) that God always respects human dignity when encountering people on an experiential level. As a consequence, if anyone should fall to the floor as an emotional response to His presence He quickly wants them up on their feet again and using their minds to relate to Him more clearly.

17) I (we) firmly deny (willingly repudiate and militantly resist) any idea that when God encounters people He wants them to: -

17:1 Lay pinned down on the floor for hours at a time, unable to move
17:2 Laugh hysterically or make animal noises
17:3 Flail around (as if having a seizure)
17:4 Stagger about (as if intoxicated by strong drink)
17:5 Jump up and down on the spot
17:6 Continue in a mindless, passive stupor

(Where such phenomena takes place the possibility of both hypnotic and demonic influences should not be ruled out.)

18) I (we) firmly deny (willingly repudiate and militantly resist) any idea that either *'love'* or *'holiness'* represent a type of metaphysical (supernatural) *'law,'* *'force'* or *'entity'* that is somehow higher in stature than God Himself. Rejected as nonsense is the belief that, *"Love is God."* Such a belief is wrong because it totally reverses the Biblical view that *"God is Love."*

19) I (we) firmly believe, (without the slightest trace of doubt or secret reservation) that God's infinite holy-love motivates all of His creative acts.

20) I (we) firmly believe, (without the slightest trace of doubt or secret reservation) that, in spite of the havoc wreaked by sin, God's holiness and love are expressed in the works of His Creation and in human affairs.

A4: MATHEMATICAL SUMMARY

The Bradford Method[59] demonstrates that: -
$\nabla(H\infty \cup L\infty) \equiv EM \neq OM \Rightarrow Re \Rightarrow Pr$ where $P\infty + \infty\sum a \Rightarrow \cup$

'The Bradford Method'[60] shows that God is a God of holy-love whose attributes of holiness and love are united by His unlimited power plus an unlimited number of other attributes. This is the equivalent of the *'essentialist model'* as distinct from the *'oppositionist model.'* Illustrated by this equation is the proposition that *"there is one holy, loving God almighty."*

In contrast, the *'oppositionist model'* errs by seeing a separation or conflict between divine holiness and divine love [Hence **OM** $\equiv \nabla(H\infty \phi L\infty)$]. The result of this model is either an over-concentration upon divine holiness, which breeds a religion of <u>fear,</u> or an over-concentration upon divine love, which breeds a religion of <u>flippancy.</u> Both produce negative *'fruits'* in people's lives (one example being a vulnerability to spiritual deception).

Hence, where **OM** $\equiv \nabla(H\infty \phi L\infty)$ a situation also arises in which
OM $\Rightarrow \nabla(H\infty - L\infty) \Rightarrow rf_1 \Rightarrow -f \supset -d$, or alternatively
OM $\Rightarrow \nabla(L\infty - H\infty) \Rightarrow rf_2 \Rightarrow -f \supset -d$

---

[59] In order not to deter the reader with seemingly off-putting equations; the decision was taken to confine *'The Bradford Method'* to the Addenda. It contains more specialised material, possibly of only little interest to those needing a more straightforward approach. This method came to mind whilst travelling by train to teach a student in Bradford during the sweltering hot afternoon of Monday, 25th May 1992. After writing it down on a scrappy piece of paper, I then re-wrote it in a notebook the following day. However, it was not incorporated into this study until Thursday, 10th February 1999.

[60] *'The Bradford Method's'* function is to highlight the relationships existing between particular biblical teachings, thereby developing a balanced view of biblical truth. Consequently, the risk of over emphasising some doctrines at the expense of others is reduced. In addition, it can contrast Biblical teachings with particular errors by showing the destructive consequences of those errors and the contradictions existing within them. It can be used in any controversy, either to defend or attack a particular position. Admittedly, this approach does presuppose a good knowledge of scripture and an ability to think in a logical way, but it serves to demonstrate how different teachings within scripture can be harmonised. If nothing else, *'The Bradford Method'* could be used to lessen the tension between such doctrines as divine holiness and love. It also has the advantage of employing theological equations to save a lot of words. As a somewhat different and unique approach, it may well prove helpful in certain instances.

Key

∇: Represents God the Holy Trinity

H∞: Infinite or unlimited divine holiness

∪: Harmonious union or unity

L∞: Infinite or unlimited divine love

≡ : The equivalent of

EM The *'essentialist model'* of divine attributes

≠ Does not equal

OM: The *'oppositionist model'* of divine attributes

Re: The divine revelation of scripture

Pr: Propositional or doctrinal statement

E.g. "there is <u>one holy, loving God</u> Almighty"

P∞: Infinite or unlimited divine power

∞∑a: unlimited sum total of other divine attributes

φ: Completely separate and distinct from

rf $_1$: A religion of <u>fear</u>

rf $_2$: A religion of <u>flippancy</u>

-f: Negative character traits and *'works of the flesh'*

-d: No defence against spiritual deception

A5: TEST SUMMARY

The following *'tests'* (methods of verification) confirm the truthfulness of the belief that the two attributes of divine holiness and love complement rather than contradict one another. These *'tests'* are: -

1) The Biblical Conformity Test
Where the belief under examination agrees with the internal evidence provided by scripture; this can clearly be seen in *'The Bible Summary'* **(Appendix 1)** and the *'Bible Expositions'* **(Chapter's 1-2)**.

2) The Coherence Test
Where the belief under examination is logically coherent and methodical as is the case in the following line of reasoning: -

2.1 The Assumption: an often unexpressed belief, idea, supposition or viewpoint based upon scripture; *i.e. God has definite attributes which can be both known and understood*
2.2 The Deduction: an openly stated belief, idea or opinion, based upon the assumption; *i.e. God's known attributes include unlimited perfection, holiness, love and power*
2.3 The Conclusion: the final evaluation or reasoned opinion that draws upon any other available information as well as the previous assumptions and deductions; i.e. *God is sufficiently perfect and powerful not to suffer any conflict between His holiness and His love*
2.4 The Application: the practical application in daily life of the reasoned conclusion; *i.e. a willingness to actively apply holy-love in our relationship with others*

3) The Compassion Test
Where the belief under examination aids believers in: -
3.1 Loving God by realising His holiness and love is all-pervading
3.2 Loving other people by realising that God can bestow a genuine care and concern for others

4) The Competitive Test
Where the belief under examination is reinforced by showing that any competing viewpoints suffer from even worse intellectual and practical problems *i.e.*
4.1 The viewpoint which overlooks divine holiness (and so cannot explain why God might seem very distant) can lead to a moral laxity, (which is one characteristic of a religion of frivolity)

4.2 The viewpoint which overlooks divine love (and so cannot explain why God should even take the time to reach out to sinful people) can lead to a moral legalism (often characterised by a religion of fear)

5) The Denial Test
Where the belief under examination is deliberately denied, ignored or misunderstood. This can lead to such intellectual and practical problems as: -
5.1 An inadequate and reduced view of God
5.2 People living as if God didn't exist at all
(Paradoxically, *'The 'Denial Test'* clearly shows that it is best not to deny the particular belief in the first place!)

6) The Dynamic Test
Where the belief under examination has the capacity to provoke constructive thought and action in different types of society; this is clearly the case with divine holiness and love, both having provoked significant, theological reflection and charitable endeavour amongst widely different societies across the ages.

7) The Evidential Test
Where the belief under examination is supplemented by external non-biblical evidence; *e.g.* in the way God uses natural phenomena like a favourable climate to provide both believers and unbelievers with the resources needed to sustain them.

8) The Explanatory Test
Where the belief under examination provides a more plausible or wider-ranging explanation than other alternatives; *e.g.* the belief in God's holy-love succinctly explains why God reveals Himself to people.

9) The Linguistic Test
Where the key words associated with the belief under examination can be clearly defined and used in a consistent way; *e.g.* divine love not being used in a way to suggest that it doesn't take into account the presence of sin

10) The Linkage Test
Where the belief under examination complements rather than contradicts another belief, by mutual cross referencing and logical connections. In particular, belief in the complementary relationship between divine holiness and divine love: -

10.1 Reinforces belief in divine omnipotence by showing that God has the power to reveal positive attributes concerning Himself

10.2 Reinforces belief in divine perfection by showing that God experiences complete inner peace (with no internal conflict existing within His innermost being)

10.3 Reinforces belief in divine zeal by showing that God is enthusiastically motivated to hold both of these attributes in perfect balance

11) The Pragmatic Test
Where the belief under examination could benefit Christians in their everyday lives; *e.g.* when an attitude of holy reverence is combined with a simple love for God provides an opportunity to witness the gospel to other people.

12) The Survival Test:
where the belief under examination survives serious opposition over a long time period whilst continuing to display *'good fruit'* in the lives of its adherents[61] (in other words, it has *'staying power'*). This is clearly the case with the teaching concerning divine holiness and divine love, which has endured repeated neglect (due to inadequate teaching) and internal church corruption, (which should ordinarily have discredited these concepts). It has survived through anything and everything.

Comments

When taken together, the above *'tests'* strongly confirm the view that the two attributes of divine holiness and divine love complement rather than contradict one another.

Therefore, it is with an intelligent, rather than a mindless faith that one can choose to accept the statement that *"There is one holy, loving God Almighty."* The future of Christianity and Messianic Judaism should prove more certain if this balance between divine holiness and divine love is firmly and wholeheartedly embraced.

---

[61] As a qualifying point, it's important to mention that it's possible for errors to endlessly propagate <u>bad</u> fruit for a very long time. A case in point is Liberal Theology, which has exerted a powerful influence in all British denominations for the last one hundred and fifty years. Other errors (like the veneration of icons) go back at least <u>fifteen hundred</u> years!

SELECTIVE BIBLIOGRAPHY

All readers are expected to use their own discernment when consulting the sources listed in this Bibliography or mentioned elsewhere in this publication. Listing in the Bibliography does not mean that the author (Raymond Creed) necessarily endorses either the content or style of these sources – nor is he responsible for the conduct or financial/legal affairs of any organization associated with them. Neither the quotation nor citation of a source in this work should be taken as a recommendation of its quality unless the author's own comments clearly suggest otherwise.

S1: Book List

Bavinck Herman (1979)
The Doctrine of God
The Banner of Truth Trust
ISBN: 085151-255-0

Brierley Peter Dr (2000)
The Tide Is Running Out
Christian Research
ISBN: 1-85321-137-0

Brierley Peter Dr (2006)
Pulling Out of the Nosedive
Christian Research
ISBN: 978-1-85321-168-3

Brown G. Callum (2001)
The Death of Christian Britain
Routledge
ISBN: 0-414-24184-7

Charnock Stephen (2000, Originally Published 1682)
The Existence and Attributes of God
Baker Books
ISBN: 0-8010-1112-4

Glover Peter (1997)
The Signs and Wonders Movement Exposed
Day One Publications
ISBN: 0902-548-751

Grudem Wayne (1994)
Systematic Theology: An Introduction to Biblical Doctrine
Inter-Varsity Press & Zondervan Publishing House
ISBN: 0-85110-652-8

Hanegraaf Hank (1993)
Christianity in Crisis
Harvest House Publishers
ISBN: 0-89081-9769

Jenkins Philip (2006)
The New Face of Christianity: Believing the Bible in the Global South
Oxford University Press
ISBN: 0-19-530065-3

Jukes Andrew (2000)
The Names of God
Kregel Publications
ISBN: 0-8254-2958-7

McDonald Elizabeth (1996)
Alpha: New Life or New Lifestyle?
St Matthew Publications
ISBN: 0:9524672-6-7

Nader Mikhaiel (1995)
Slaying In the Spirit: The Telling Wonder
Southward Press
ISBN: 0-646-12574-5

Packer J. I. (1978)
Knowing God
Hodder and Stoughton
ISBN: 0-340-1913-7

Pink W. Arthur (2001)
The Attributes of God
Baker Book House Company
ISBN: 0-8010-6989-0

Sparrow Giles (2006)
Cosmos: A Field Guide
Quercus
ISBN: 1-905204-29-9

Tozer A. W. (1976)
The Knowledge of the Holy
Send the Light Trust

S2: Reference Works

Augustine of Hippo (1991)
Saint Augustine: Volume V, Writings against the Pelagians
T & T Clark Eerdmans Publishing USA
ISBN: 0-567-09394-8 & 0-8028-8102-5

Brierley Peter Dr – Editor (2003)
UK Handbook, Religious Trends 4
Christian Research
ISBN: 1-85321-149-4

Brierley Peter Dr – Editor (2005)
UK Handbook, Religious Trends 5
Christian Research
ISBN: 1-85321-160-5

Douglas D J – Editor (1978)
The New International Dictionary of the Christian Church
The Paternoster Press Ltd
(By arrangement with Zondervan Corporation USA)
ISBN: 0-85364-221-4

Ferguson B. Sinclair & Wright F. David (1988)
New Dictionary of Theology
Inter-Varsity Press
ISBN: 0-855110-636-6

Fisher-Park George (1927)
History of Christian Doctrine
Edinburgh T & T Clark

Lane Tony (1992)
The Lion Book of Christian Thought
Lion Publishing PLC
ISBN: 0-7324-0575-0

S3: Other Information Sources

These have included various private contacts whose names cannot be disclosed for reasons of confidentially. Also, video footage of some Television Programmes dating from the mid-1990s concerning the Toronto Experience and many news bulletins from *'The Christian Institute'* at http://www.christian.org.uk

TITLES BY THE SAME AUTHOR

NOTICE

For information on the ordering and pricing of these titles please visit
http://stores.lulu.com/rebuildchristianity or

http://stores.lulu.com/store.php?fAcctID=976144

For information on their contents and for sample extracts please visit the author's website at
www.rebuildchristianity.com/L1.htm

For other publications by the author please visit
www.rebuildchristianity.com

For contact details please visit
www.rebuildchristianity.com/L5.htm#co

Soft cover versions of these titles should be available through Amazon and other International Distributors.

In the event of any difficulty with these *'links'* please search using the *'Book Title' and* the name *'Raymond Creed.'* Doing this should access a relevant site.

FACING THE UNTHINKABLE

'Facing the Unthinkable' dramatically portrays the likely emotional and psychological reactions of a beleaguered number of Jewish people at the very point when they turn to their true Messiah. Their state of near-total despair will suddenly change to one of exuberant joy. Following their recognition and acceptance of the Messiah all of the bible prophecies concerning the restoration of Israel will begin to be fulfilled.

'Facing the Unthinkable' provides hope for the Messianic Jewish Community and for those Christians with a genuine interest in the Jewish people. It helps rebuild Christianity by emphasising its links to both Israel and Judaism.

Great care is taken to address the following questions: -
1) How will the Jewish people come to believe in their true Messiah?
2) How will they react when they encounter Him?
3) How will the world react to this unexpected development?

This book breaks new ground in its creative expression of the spiritual and psychological aspects likely to be experienced when the true Messiah is recognised. It's assumed that both the nation of Israel and the whole of humanity itself will be on the brink of annihilation before this unique event happens. G-d will have allowed much suffering to have taken place to show man's abject failure in his attempt to create a New World Order. The promise of a better and fairer world will have been cruelly exposed and falsified.

'Facing the Unthinkable' is an invaluable resource for those engaged in any form of Jewish work or who have a sympathetic interest in the State of Israel. It may be regarded as an independent work or as a successor volume to *'The Leeds Liturgy.'*

To purchase a download, hard or soft cover edition please visit: -

http://stores.lulu.com/rebuildchristianity or

http://stores.lulu.com/store.php?fAcctID=976144

Soft cover editions may also be available through Amazon and other International Distributors.

THE 52 ATTRIBUTES OF GOD

'The 52 Attributes of God' explores God's unique character. It uses ancient Jewish methods of bible interpretation (*'Midrash'*) along with prayerful meditations, proverbial sayings and simple summaries. Each chapter combines both analytical with devotional material and readers are encouraged to progress at their own pace. *'The 52 Attributes of God'* is readily accessible for both private and group use and employs a stimulating variety of questions to aid reflection and to encourage practical application. It shows how all 52 of the divine attributes were displayed during Christ's death and it helps rebuild Christianity by using *'Midrash'* to provide a clearer picture of God's nature.

Great care is taken to answer such questions as: -
1) Who is God?
2) What is He like?
3) How did He react to the death of His Son Jesus?
4) How does He react to the corruption found within much of today's Church?
5) To what extent can we become like God?

'The 52 Attributes of God' should prove particularly useful to religious ministers (of all denominational backgrounds), local church elders, Christian teachers, evangelists and theological students. The Messianic Jewish community and those wishing to delve deeper into theology would especially benefit. Any public or academic library with a theological section will find it a rich resource. It should also be of assistance to those confused or troubled by particular *'spiritualities'* which alluringly offer the chance to become divine.

This book ends by warning that those choosing to ignore the clear distinction between God and Man (by presuming they have a right to become mini-gods) often end up behaving like devils.

To purchase a download, hard or soft cover edition please visit: -

http://stores.lulu.com/rebuildchristianity or

http://stores.lulu.com/store.php?fAcctID=976144

Soft cover editions may also be available through Amazon and other International Distributors.

THE LEEDS LITURGY

The Leeds Liturgy' encourages Christians to worship God *"in spirit and in truth"* (John 4:24). In terms of doctrine, it aspires to be the truest and most accurate book outside of scripture. Its pages contain *'The Leeds Creed'* which is the most comprehensive creedal *'Statement of Faith'* in Christianity to date, (Acts 20:27). This *'statement'* integrates bible-based insights from every Christian Tradition and provides a comprehensive summary of those doctrines needed for salvation and for effective Christian living. Also included are revised versions of the Apostles, Nicene and Athanasian Creeds.

'The Leeds Liturgy' aims to: -
1) Provide a legacy of truth for present and future believers
2) Testify to the one true Gospel that *"Jesus Christ came into the world to save sinners,"* (I Timothy 1:15b)
3) Portray doctrine in a fresh, interactive and understandable way
4) Promote an exuberant style of worship
5) Declare the *'whole counsel [full teaching] of God'* to a Church that currently seems to value everything else but the teaching of Scripture
6) Enable believers (largely due to its provision of sound doctrinal teaching) to better withstand persecution and hardship
7) Bring Jew and Gentile together in joint worship of the one true God of Israel
8) Nurture the community life of Messianic Jewish and Christian groups
9) Offer a distinctive way of presenting timeless truths to a sinful world
10) Enable believers to interact with bible teaching (either individually or in a group setting)

'The Leeds Liturgy' proclaims the Gospel by pointing to Christ as the only means whereby eternal life is received. His full deity and full humanity are equally emphasised – as is the Trinitarian relationship between Himself, His Father and the Holy Spirit. Christians are encouraged to relate to these Persons through the material provided in this resource. It attempts to be a vehicle with the innate capacity to be used by the Holy Spirit, who eagerly wants to lead Christians into all truth, (John 16:13a). It highlights the fact that, in order to place our faith in God, we must first of all lose faith in ourselves.

'The Leeds Liturgy' closes with two articles exploring the biblical roots of Liturgies and Creeds. These could be of particular interest to students working in the field of liturgical studies. Its successor volume,

'Facing the Unthinkable' provides a dramatic anticipation of how Israel will recognize the true messiah during a period of great affliction.

To purchase a download, hard or soft cover edition please visit: -

http://stores.lulu.com/rebuildchristianity or

http://stores.lulu.com/store.php?fAcctID=976144

Soft cover versions may also be available through Amazon and other International Distributors.

NOTES

www.ingramcontent.com/pod-product-compliance
Lightning Source LLC
Chambersburg PA
CBHW022108160426
43198CB00008B/392